CHRISTIAN MORALITY

James Nelson and Juliana McNeice

Colourpoint

© James Nelson
Juliana McNeice
1998

ISBN 0 898392 45 5

8 7 6 5 4 3 2 1

Layout and design: Colourpoint Books
Cover design: Barry Craig for Colourpoint
Printed by: ColourBooks

Colourpoint Books
Unit D5 Ards Business Centre
Jubilee Road
NEWTOWNARDS
Co Down
BT23 4YH

Tel: 01247 820505
Fax: 01247 821900
E-mail: info@colourpoint.co.uk

The Authors

James Nelson teaches Religious Studies and English in Regent House Grammar School in Newtownards, Co Down. He has a BEd and an MA in Religious Studies.

Juliana McNeice is Head of Religious Studies in Rainey Endowed School, Magherafelt, Co Londonderry. She has a BEd in Religious Studies.

Picture credits
Getty Images 10, 21, 23, 28, 34, 38, 42, 49, 55, 58
Kobal Collection 5, 20, 31, 32, 45, 62, 68
Universal Pictorial Press 36
Malcolm Johnston 69, 73, 78
Norman Johnston 6, 24, 48, 50, 72
Sheila Johnston 46
Barry Craig 35, 71
All copyright has been acknowledged to the best of our ability. We apologise for any inadvertant omissions, which we shall endeavour to correct in any future editions.

Colourpoint is indebted to the Leprosy Mission for kindly supplying the picture of Diana, Princess of Wales, on page 8.
Grateful thanks also to the Salvation Army for the picture on page 53.
The Salvation Army has a Schools and Colleges Information Service which produces a schools pack and other resources. Contact 0171 3320022 ext 2112
Extracts on page 13 are from
Across the Barricades
by Joan Lingard, Penguin, 1973

Contents

INTRODUCTION

The primary intention of this book is to provide a resource for Religious Studies which directly meets the needs of the Christian Morality section of the Northern Ireland Core Syllabus at Key Stage 4. It is hoped that it lends itself to creative and interactive classroom practice and that a use may also be found for it in non-school contexts such as youth groups and church organisations.

We have tried to go beyond a general discussion of the issues to explore, where relevant, the teaching of the four main Churches in Ireland. In all cases we have tried to represent each Church accurately and we would like to thank the representatives of the Churches who assisted us in this:

Father Martin O'Hagan, St. Matthew's Roman Catholic Church, Belfast.
Rev D. Cooper, Knock Methodist Church.
Norman Chambers, Presbyterian Board of Social Witness.
Liz Gibson-Harries (Press Officer) and Canon Turner, Church of Ireland.

We would also like to thank Kate Nixon for her legal expertise, Brendan Gerard for his knowledgeable corrections, and to Relate (Northern Ireland), Accord, Churches in Co-operation, The Leprosy Mission, The Salvation Army, Ballymena YMCA, The Simon Community, The National Foster Care Campaign and The Health Promotion Agency (Northern Ireland) for their permission to use material.

Of course a very special thanks to Colourpoint for their excellent work and, in particular, Sheila for her gentle, steady directing.

James Nelson and **Juliana McNeice**, June 1998

All Biblical references are taken from *The Good News Bible* unless stated otherwise

The following symbols are used throughout the book to guide the reader in finding particular references:

 Discussion

 Activity

 Questions

 Church references

 Biblical references

FRIENDSHIP

What is a friend?

"A true friend is one who sticks by you even when he gets to know you real well."
J McKenzie

We relate to people on many different levels. Someone may simply be a *colleague*, that is, a person we work with or sit beside at school. An *acquaintance* is someone we may see on a regular basis without necessarily knowing them in a deep or meaningful way — perhaps a person who goes to the same football club. *Peers* are people who are equal to us in age or status.

The people we call our *close friends* are usually a smaller group of people with whom we are more intimate. They are the ones with whom we can share our successes and failures, our hurts and our happiness. We tell our deepest secrets to the best of our friends. Even though they can sometimes annoy us, they are still the people who matter to us the most.

Making friends

"The only reward of virtue is virtue; the only way to have a friend is to be one."
Ralph Waldo Emerson

There are no categories and no rules when it comes to talking about how friendships are made. Some happen instantly, others evolve. Some people make friends easily, others find it more difficult. But the most important thing about making friends is that you cannot be forced into it — only

'Friends' US TV series

FRIENDSHIP SEXUALITY & RESPONSIBILITY

"Of all the things which provide to make life entirely happy, much the greatest is the possession of friendship."
Epicurus

During your childhood and teenage years you will already have had a wide experience of forming relationships with a variety of people. Try to think about how many friends you have made, or lost since you started primary school — probably more than you thought. Developing friendships is an essential part of growing up. It helps us to become independent and to establish relationships outside our family. You may like to have one or two close friends of your own age, or you may meet regularly with a mixed age-group of people. Perhaps you prefer your friends to like the same music as you or to go to the same places at weekends. All friendships and relationships are unique.

you can decide who your friends are. You may not be able to choose your family, but you can choose your friends. Here are some important factors which help us when choosing our friends:

◆ Common interests / different interests
◆ Feeling comfortable with a person
◆ Character / personality
◆ Trust
◆ Loyalty
◆ Commitment

Can you think of any others?

When choosing your friends it is important to choose wisely. You may call a person your friend but, in reality, they may not be loyal to you and you may not be able to trust them. Also, friends could lead you into behaving in a way which you don't like, or that you know is wrong, but a true friend should respect your opinions and not tempt you into something which could be dangerous or could get you into trouble.

For some people, making friends can be a very difficult and painful experience. Perhaps they are simply shy or feel reluctant to become close to others. Some may have a low self-esteem because they have been teased or bullied. Others may have had the experience of being hurt by friends in the past. For these individuals, friendships might seem to be more work than they are worth, but having close relationships with others is usually a rewarding experience. Friendships help us to grow as people. We gain self-confidence from shared experience; our attitudes and beliefs can change or be strengthened as a result of the influence of a friend. Some friendships last a lifetime and can bring great happiness.

Discussion

1 **In groups discuss:**
   a) How important are your friends to you? Are you friendly with a wide range of people or do you have just a few very close friends? Do you think you are a good friend?
   b) Try to make a list of the qualities you think make a good friend and put them in order of importance to you.

Activity

Write a letter to a friend (you don't have to put his or her name on it or send it) explaining the positive qualities that they have and why you enjoy their friendship.
                    OR
Write a poem which explores the qualities found in a good friend.

What the Bible says

Christians believe that they have a duty to show friendship to all people. Jesus led by example; he befriended dozens of people including those whom the religious leaders called 'sinners' — cheats, prostitutes, and lepers. In his teaching Jesus leaves Christians in no doubt about the depth of significance which friendships can have:

"Love each other as I have loved you. Greater love has no-one than this, that one lay down his life for his friends."

                              John 15: 12-13

In the **Old Testament** the virtues of good friendship are mentioned frequently. Many are written as proverbs:

"Two are better than one, because they have a good return for their work: If one falls down his friend can help him up. But pity the man who falls and has no-one to help him up."

                              Ecclesiastes 4: 9-10

"A friend loves at all times and a brother is born of adversity."

                              Proverbs 17:17

One of the best known examples of friendship in the Bible is that of David and Jonathan.

Read 1 Samuel 20

David and Jonathan are young men who are the best of friends. Jonathan's father is King Saul who in his older age has become mentally unstable. At times he is filled with seething hatred for David and on other occasions he treats him with kindness, almost like a son. In this passage Jonathan's loyalties are divided, yet he is determined to be a true friend to David no matter how difficult the circumstances.

Discussion

1 **In what way might young people today experience divided loyalties between their parents and their friends?**
2 **How might the Bible give direction or guidance in such a situation?**

Christians tend to have strong friendships with others who share the same faith. The reasons for this are obviously because they share a lot of the same interests. For example, they meet regularly at church worship and other social activities. However, Christian friendship is more than just sharing common interests. It is a bond which comes from a shared faith. This means that Christians spend time listening to and learning from each other, sharing their concerns, problems and joys as well as discussing their relationship with God. When Christians express their friendship in this way it is sometimes called having **fellowship.** Christians believe that fellowship is also an expression of obedience to God's command to 'love one another'. But this Christian friendship also has a practical side. It is not enough, only to *listen* to your friends' problems, it is essential to offer practical assistance as well. This can range from showing hospitality to giving financial assistance through a church collection.

Broken friendships

"A man, Sir, should keep his friendship in constant repair."

Dr Samuel Johnson

All friendships have their ups and downs. Indeed those closest to us can often hurt us the most. We are open with them and, therefore,

more vulnerable. This means that when friends fall out it can have a profound effect on each of them and can even end the relationship. For example, someone may betray your trust or let you down. When this happens you may feel that you cannot forgive them or ever speak to them in a friendly way again. The Bible teaches:

"If you become angry, do not let your anger lead you into sin, and do not stay angry all day."
Ephesians 4: 26

This suggests that when friends do argue they should try to resolve the situation as quickly as possible. Obviously it will take time to heal all the hurt but the longer the fighting or silence goes on the more difficult things become. Christians also believe that the practice of forgiveness is essential in all relationships and, occasionally, it is necessary to accept someone else's faults and forget about trying to blame them.

Of course there are other reasons why some friendships fail — friends may simply grow apart, or one may move house or school and the friendship dies naturally.

Questions

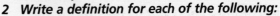

1 **Read 1 John 3: 18. Explain what it teaches about Christian love or friendship.**
2 **Write a definition for each of the following:**
   • **colleague**
   • **acquaintance**
   • **peers**
4 **Using clear examples from the Bible explain what is meant by 'Christian friendship'.**
5 **Do you think Christians have difficulty making friends with non-Christians? Give reasons for your answer.**
6 **a) Give two reasons why friendship ends.**
   b) How might this experience be painful?
7 **"Friends, companions, lovers are those who treat us in terms of our unlimited worth to ourselves. They are closest to us, who feel for us as we feel for ourselves, who are bound to us in triumph and disaster, who break the spell of our loneliness" (Henry Alonzo Myers). Look at this quotation and the others throughout this chapter. Then try to write your own statement on friendship.**
8 **If you choose your friends badly, what possible dangers or problems might it lead to? Give three examples.**

Activity

a It is common for groups of young Christians to attend fellowship weekends or retreats. Try to record an interview with someone you know who has been on such a weekend. Make a list of interview questions and try to find out how the group showed their friendship to each other and in what ways they shared in fellowship? Present your findings to the rest of the class.

b Look at the following letters to a 'problem' page and write your own reply.

I'm Lonely

"Dear Linda,
I'm a girl of 18 and I've just started university and I'm really miserable because I miss my home and friends. Everyone else seems to have loads of confidence and I feel lonely and left out."

Snubbed

"Dear Linda,
Two years ago I became friendly with a new girl to our school. At first she didn't really fit in but when I got to know her better she turned out to be really good fun. I introduced her to my circle of friends who went out of their way to make her feel welcome. Recently I discovered that she has organised a party but hasn't invited me. I feel really 'gutted' by this and don't know if I can forgive her."

Diana, Princess of Wales, at Sitanala Hospital, Indonesia. Even though she was a Princess and didn't need to worry about the problems of poverty, disease and injustice, she was determined to show love to others by comforting, encouraging, and caring for them.

Love

For centuries poets, songwriters and authors have tried to define love or to express the emotions which accompany it, yet there never seem to be enough words to explain what love is.

What is love?

"It is an ever fixed-mark that looks on tempests, and is never shaken."

W Shakespeare

"Love is a universal migraine, a bright stain on the vision blotting out reason."

Robert Graves

"Love is fish and chips on winter nights."

Adrian Henri

Try to find some other famous quotations about love.

In our society 'love' is a word that can mean many different things. Think of the books you read, the songs you listen to, the conversations you have with your friends. How many times is the word 'love' mentioned and what does it mean in each circumstance? Look at the following statements and try to explain what the word 'love' means in each one.

"I love dance music and clubbing."
"My family loves me deeply."
"I've fallen in love!"
"And so we know and rely on the love God has for us. God is love." (1 John 4: 16)

Type of love	Greek word	Meaning
Affection	Storge	'Liking something'; it could mean liking objects, hobbies, jobs, places or animals. Between people it means 'getting on well together'.
Sexual	Eros	1. Physical attraction for another person. Animal passion for sex. 2. Falling in love. Feeling that there is no-one quite like the other person.
Friendship/ Family	Philos	A deep friendship which is one part of your life. It may be based on a common interest or bond.
Christian	Agapé	A practical love which requires effort. Based on a respect for all people. Accepting someone unconditionally.

Some people think that because the word 'love' is used so often and in so many different ways that it has lost any true meaning. Do you agree? One way we can try to understand the different types of love is by looking at the Greek language which distinguishes between four different kinds of love. These are explained in the panel above.

Questions

1   **Look back to the four sentences about love that we started with (eg "I love dance music and clubbing"). Write out each one and instead of the word 'love' write the Greek word which best describes the type of love meant there.**
2   **Now make up four of your own sentences with 'love' in them using a Greek word in its place.**

What the Bible says

The word 'love' is constantly referred to throughout the Bible and it is, arguably, its greatest theme. It would be impossible to list all the verses which mention love but several passages can give us a good indication of what the Bible has to say about this topic.

One of the teachers of the law came and heard them debating. Noticing that Jesus had given them a good answer, he asked him, "Of all the commandments, which is the most important?" "The most important one," answered Jesus, "is this: `Hear, O Israel, the Lord our God, the Lord is one. Love the Lord your God with all your heart and with all your soul and with all your mind and with all your strength.' The second is this: `Love your neighbour as yourself.' There is no commandment greater than these."

Mark 12: 28-31

Dear friends, let us love one another, for love comes from God. Everyone who loves has been born of God and knows God. Whoever does not love does not know God, because God is love. This is how God showed his love among us: He sent his one and only Son into the world that we might live through him. This is love: not that we loved God, but that he loved us and sent his Son as an atoning sacrifice for our sins. Dear friends, since God so loved us, we also ought to love one another. No one has ever seen God; but if we love one another, God lives in us and his love is made complete in us.

1 John 4: 7-12

In the next passage about love the apostle Paul is writing to a church in the city of Corinth explaining to them how to worship and how to treat one another properly. There were those in the church who believed that the more active they were in leading the worship, preaching, speaking in tongues or even enduring hardships

9

for being Christians, then the better and more spiritual they were. Paul points out that all of these things may seem good in themselves but the really important thing is the reason *why* they are done. If they are done for selfish reasons or as a way of gaining popularity or power they are worthless and pointless in God's eyes. Paul believes that, in everything, Christians should act humbly, honestly and selflessly — in short they should always be motivated by love (agapé).

1 Corinthians 13: 1-13 (New International Version)

If I speak in the tongues of men and of angels, but have not love, I am only a resounding gong or a clanging cymbal. If I have the gift of prophecy and can fathom all mysteries and all knowledge, and if I have a faith that can move mountains, but have not love, I am nothing. If I give all I possess to the poor and surrender my body to the flames, but have not love, I gain nothing. Love is patient, love is kind. It does not envy, it does not boast, it is not proud. It is not rude, it is not self-seeking, it is not easily angered, it keeps no record of wrongs. Love does not delight in evil but rejoices with the truth. It always protects, always trusts, always hopes, always perseveres. Love never fails. But where there are prophecies, they will cease; where there are tongues, they will be stilled; where there is knowledge, it will pass away. For we know in part and we prophesy in part, but when perfection comes, the imperfect disappears. When I was a child, I talked like a child, I thought like a child, I reasoned like a child. When I became a man, I put childish ways behind me. Now we see but a poor reflection as in a mirror; then we shall see face to face. Now I know in part; then I shall know fully, even as I am fully known. And now these three remain: faith, hope and love. But the greatest of these is love.

This is one of the most famous passages in the Bible and in many ways summarises what the Christian attitude to life should be about. It was read at the funeral of Diana, Princess of Wales, by the Prime Minister Tony Blair. Even though she was a Princess and didn't need to worry about the problems of poverty, disease and injustice, she was determined to show love to others by comforting, encouraging, and caring for them.

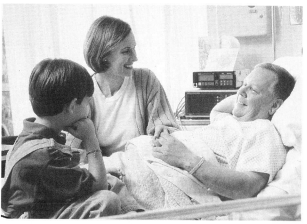

The Christian Church: a community of love

According to the Apostles' Creed, Christians believe in:

"The holy, catholic church, the communion of saints ..."

This means a church which is worldwide (catholic), which is set apart for God's work (holy) and the members of which are united in a fellowship of love with one another (communion of saints).

The picture of the early church in the book of Acts also gives a clear example of the church as a loving community:

"All the believers continued together in close fellowship and shared their belongings with one another. They would sell their property and possessions, and distribute the money among all, according to what each one needed. Day after day they met in the Temple, and they had their meals together in their homes, eating with glad and humble hearts, praising God, and enjoying the good will of all the people."

Acts 2: 44-47

Today Christians still strive to create loving communities in their churches, although this generally doesn't involve living a totally communal lifestyle like the first Christians. Some churches emphasise the importance of worshipping together in a spirit of love. For others the stress falls more on love as a practical action which is shown in the community in which they live. However, all churches agree that their aim is to attempt to live a life of *agapé* love. Here are just a few simple examples of how love is practiced in a church community:

- a group of young people singing carols in an old person's home;
- offering the 'sign of peace' at a worship service;
- giving money to charity;
- visiting someone in hospital;
- comforting those who are bereaved.

Love: A guiding principle

Look back at the Bible reference Mark 12: 28-31. When Jesus gave the commandment to love one another he meant it as *a guiding principle for all of life*. He said it was the greatest commandment because if you treat people and God with love then you will fulfil the ten commandments. So all Christian behaviour should be governed by this '**love principle**'. It is perhaps easier to understand the significance of Christ's teaching by comparing it to the ideas of other famous thinkers.

In the fourth century BC a philosopher called **Epicurus** said that a good life was one which was dedicated to the pursuit of *pleasure*:

"For we recognize pleasure as the primary and natural desire, and we return to it in all our judgements of the good, taking the feeling of pleasure as our guide."

from The Letter to Menoeceus

Aristotle, another Greek philosopher, argued that "a life of pleasure is only fit for animals" and that the only way to act properly and be happy was by living a *virtuous life*. Human beings are not born with virtues, they must be taught them, but once they learn how to be fair, courageous, honest and noble they will then know what is right to do.

Jeremy Bentham and John Stuart Mill in the eighteenth century said that the only way to decide what was right or wrong was by considering whether an action would bring pleasure or pain, but this was not just a decision for the individual. According to Bentham and Mill, you should always do whatever brings "*the greatest happiness to the greatest number of people*". This is called Utilitarianism.

A German philosopher, **Immanuel Kant**, said that we act morally if we ignore our own desires and do our *moral duty*. To help us find out what our moral duty is in any situation you must ask yourself "Would I wish that my action be made a universal law?" If not, then it is wrong. So, for

example, it is wrong to break a promise because you would not wish it to become the norm — otherwise no-one would trust anyone else.

In the 1960s an idea developed that there are *no moral absolutes*; in other words no action is ever completely right or completely wrong, it depends on the circumstances. In some cases stealing is wrong but there could be occasions when stealing is morally the right thing to do — for example, is it right to steal a loaf of bread to feed starving children? This teaching came to be known as **situation ethics**.

In contrast to these moral viewpoints Jesus teaches that:

a) there are **absolute moral values** (things which are always right or always wrong) based on the principle of love, some of which can be expressed as rules (for example, the Ten Commandments), which should be applied in every situation.

b) to act out of love is to show care, honour, fairness and forgiveness to all people in all situations; that is to **treat all human beings with dignity and respect**.

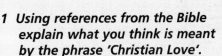

Questions

1 **Using references from the Bible explain what you think is meant by the phrase 'Christian Love'.**
2 **In what ways can Christians put this love into practice in their everyday lives?**
3 **Do you think 'love one another' is enough as a rule for life?**

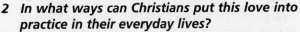

Activity

Imagine you are stranded on a desert island with a group of four or five friends. You have a few supplies including a knife, rope, matches, a compass and some plastic bags.
a) **Firstly try to establish your plan for survival.**
b) **Now decide how you will make decisions. Will you appoint a leader or take a vote on every decision?**
c) **Try to draw up five rules for your island.**
d) **Finally, discuss whether you could live by only one rule: 'Love your neighbour as you love yourself'. Consider the pros and cons.**

BOY - GIRL RELATIONSHIPS

When you enter your teenage years relationships tend to include those with members of the opposite sex. Physical attraction often initiates this type of relationship but friendship and common interests are needed to sustain it.

Emotions are sometimes hard to comprehend when it comes to a relationship with a member of the opposite sex. For example, you may think that you have fallen in love with someone you don't even know; this is called **infatuation**. Or you may feel you love someone simply because you feel a strong physical desire for them but this is only **lust**. Love involves much more; it requires real knowledge of the other person, to be able to see beyond their good looks or expensive car, and to cope with them when they're at their worst.

Activity

Look at the following list of qualities. Which of these would you consider the most important in a boyfriend or girlfriend? Give reasons for your choice.

Trustworthy	Same religion	Tolerant
Good looking	Sense of humour	Good communicator
Likes your friends	Common interests	Wealthy
Parents approve	Similar views	Popular
Good manners	Considerate	Romantic
Generous	Friendly	Sensitive

Can you think of any others?

Discussion: Relationships in focus

In groups read the following questions and discuss:
1 **What are the pressures on teenagers when it comes to relationships?**
2 **What expectations do you think the opposite sex have of you?**
3 **Complete the following phrase "Boys/Girls would be so much easier to have relationships with, if...."**

From your discussion you will have confirmed your suspicions that finding a boyfriend or girlfriend, and going out with them, isn't always simple and straightforward. Indeed, it would be easy to fall into the trap of thinking that making and maintaining relationships is something that just happens to the lucky ones, but those who study behaviour are convinced that there are skills which can be learnt, which enhance our ability to have successful relationships. Look at the following suggestions and in groups try to add some more:
◆ be positive about yourself;
◆ take time to listen to what the other person has to say;
◆ avoid fighting and try to compromise.

What the Bible says

In today's culture male-female relationships are very different from anything that happened during the Biblical period. In those days people didn't 'go out' with each other and so it was not unusual for girls to be betrothed by the age of twelve (at this age they were officially adults) and married by the time they were fifteen. However, the Bible is still able to offer some advice on relationships. For example, in the story of Ruth and Boaz in the **Old Testament** we see the importance of perseverance, self-confidence and trust in God when choosing a partner.

Read Ruth 3: 1-18

Another very important part of growing up and developing relationships is learning to deal with feelings of insecurity or lack of confidence with our bodies or even feelings of worthlessness because a certain person doesn't like us. Running right throughout the Bible is the theme that each individual person is valued and loved by God. This is important when involved in any kind of relationship. In the Old Testament Psalm 139 outlines God's interest and care for each individual:

"You are all around me on every side; you protect me with your power. Your knowledge of me is too deep: it is beyond my understanding."

Psalm 139: 5-6

Similarly in the **New Testament** Jesus explains how precious each person is in the eyes of God:

"For only a penny you can buy two sparrows, yet not one sparrow falls to the ground without your Father's consent. As for you, even the hairs of your head have all been counted. So do not be afraid; you are worth much more than many sparrows!"

Matthew 10: 29-31

Christians believe it is important to strive to maintain a similar outlook in our everyday relationships and treatment of others.

Below is a magazine article designed to give advice to teenagers about boy-girl relationships:

Going Out

Asking someone out and going out with them can be enjoyable, exciting, and fulfilling but it can also be difficult, awkward and embarrassing at times. Here we try to offer you some practical advice on finding a suitable partner, what to expect and how to make your relationships a success. To help you see how it can be done we've included a few extracts from **Across The Barricades,** a novel set in Belfast about a Protestant girl, Sadie, and a Catholic boy, Kevin, who fall in love. In an early scene in the book the two are looking over Belfast Lough from Cave Hill:

It was peaceful up there on the hill with the wind playing round their faces and tousling their hair. Sadie sat with her knees up to her chin, hugging her legs. She felt at ease with Kevin, though of course it was seldom she felt ill-at-ease with anybody, but she also felt a sort of contentment that she was unused to.
"It's funny," she began.
"What?" He turned on one elbow to look at her.
"I was just thinking a place looks better if you've got somebody with you."
"Two pairs of eyeballs are better than one. As long as they're the right two pairs of course."
He has a sweet tongue on him, she thought. He was gazing back down at the city again. She stole a look at him.

His face was not very broad but it was firm and had a suggestion of strength about it; it was also deeply tanned with the look of one who was seldom indoors. He probably went home only to sleep. She understood the feeling of restlessness in him. She had it herself.

Just good friends?

At this stage in the book Sadie and Kevin are just good friends and it is not until later that they become boyfriend and girlfriend. It is not uncommon for a boy-girl friendship to develop into romance. In fact it is perhaps a healthy sign if the relationship is built on a sound friendship. Shared interests, time spent talking together, having a laugh and trusting each other should be part of a boy-girl relationship. You could say that being with a girlfriend or boyfriend is not very far removed from being with other good friends.

Talking together

To become friendly with someone it is obviously essential to talk to them. Some people do feel shy when it comes to talking to someone whom they find attractive. It is best to avoid silly chat-up lines, or having another person to do the asking for you. There is no better way than to make your own feelings felt in your own way and in your own time. Of course, don't go to the other extreme of talking non-stop. You need to relax, be yourself and remember that the key to a good conversation is knowing how to listen.

Picking a location

Cave Hill is not everyone's idea of paradise and you may not get far by suggesting that your first date be at the top of a mountain! But it is important to go somewhere you can spend time with each other in an environment you both enjoy. You may prefer to meet at a club or café or to go for a walk along the beach. Perhaps you would want to go out in a large group but it is important to spend some time alone together. Back to Kevin and Sadie:

"Well," said Kevin lightly, jumping to his feet, "will we go?" He held out his hand to her.
They walked down the hill close together but not touching. Lights were springing up in the houses, the blue in the sky was deepening and changing. Every moment it looked different; new colours and shades merged and infiltrated the blue : pinks, yellows, turquoise, red.
"Look at the sky," said Sadie. She felt she had never seen a sky before.
They stopped to look at it and Kevin rested a hand on her shoulder. His hand was warm and she liked the feel of it.
"It's a fair sight," said Kevin. "You never see it properly from the street." He held her hand as they descended the last part of the hill and kept hold of it once they had reached the bottom.

Physical contact

Going out on a date doesn't mean that there must be intimate physical contact. Some boys believe that if a girl agrees to go on a date she is giving her consent to physical contact and he can expect to be kissed at the very least. But going out with someone is not about satisfying your sex-drive. It is about building a relationship with another person. As you get to know them better, learn to trust them and feel closer to them, a physical relationship will develop in a way which keeps pace with the rest of the relationship.

Activity

Design an article for a Christian teenage magazine (like the one on page 17) with the title "A guide to successful relationships". Include relevant quotations from the Bible. Use the headings below to help you plan your work.
- Choosing a boy-friend or girl-friend
- Asking them out
- Going out
- Facing problems
- Making it last or ending it

Coping with problems

Young people may have several boy/girl-friends during their teenage years. This means that they will have to go through the unfortunate and sometimes traumatic process of splitting up. The reasons why couples may split-up include:
- the person you liked from a distance is not as attractive when you get to know them better;
- the relationship might come under unbearable pressure from friends or family;
- you or your partner might find another person who appeals to you more;
- you may feel too young to be committed to one person and you need your own space.

When a couple begin to have difficulties it needn't be inevitable that the relationship ends. No couple ever lives in perfect bliss all the time and it is important to learn how to cope with problems when they arise rather than simply running away from the relationship. Working to solve the problems may mean that a breakup can be avoided.

Mending a relationship requires a couple to speak openly, maturely and to listen attentively to what the other person has to say. Successful relationships are not those which are problem-free but those which cope effectively with problems when they arise. One strategy that the Bible recommends is to deal quickly with problems as they arise:

"If you become angry, do not let your anger lead you into sin, and do not stay angry all day."

Ephesians 4: 26

Another important aspect of mending relationships is forgiveness. This is a constant theme in all of Christ's teaching and St Paul also reminds Christians to:

"Be kind and tender-hearted to one another, and forgive one another, as God has forgiven you."

Ephesians 4: 32

If a break-up is unavoidable, Christians believe that it should be handled maturely and without bitterness, so that feelings of anger or revenge do not take over. Although it is never pleasant, a separation may be a learning experience which helps you understand your own emotions better.

Discussion

1 What do you think are the most common reasons for teenage relationships breaking up?
2 Do you think it is important to try to work at a relationship if it experiences difficulties? Give some practical suggestions how a couple might mend a relationship in which one partner is angry with the other because they are not spending enough time together.

Questions

1 In your opinion is the Bible out-of-date regarding advice about relationships? Give reasons for your answer.
2 Why is it important to have other friends as well as a boy/girl friend?
3 Imagine you are a leader in a church youth group and a teenager has asked your advice on how to act during a first date. With reference to Christian values, explain what you would say.
4 A healthy relationship requires a balance of friendship, love and physical attraction. What dangers are there if physical attraction is the only component?

Appreciation of Sexuality

Sexuality is an important part of being human. Our primary identifying characteristic is our gender — we are born either masculine or feminine. Also, we all have a sexual nature which is linked to our emotional and psychological needs. In order to understand sexuality it is important to put our misconceived ideas and prejudices to one side and consider the whole area with an open mind.

Sexual identity and sexual stereotypes

An advertisement from the 1950s. What do you think of it?

What does it mean to be male or female in our society? Was it different 20, 50, or 100 years ago? Are there 'male jobs' or 'female jobs'? Do women have different emotions to men? The answers to these questions can help us understand what we mean when we talk about our sexual or gender identity. As we grow up we develop physical characteristics, habits, attitudes and skills which are part of being male or female. Some of these we develop naturally but some we acquire from the society in which we live. It has always been hotly debated which characteristics are natural and which are a result of social conditioning. For example, are men naturally better leaders than women or are there more male managers and directors because women aren't brought up to believe that they possess the qualities and characteristics of leadership?

Sexual stereotyping occurs when we assume a person to have certain characteristics simply because they are male or female — for example, "Women are good at domestic tasks" or "Men enjoy talking about football and cars". Stereotyping is dangerous because it encourages us to judge others and not to allow people to act as individuals.

In recent times, male and female roles have changed dramatically. This has been largely due to the **Women's Movement** (also known as **Women's Liberation** and the **Feminist Movement**). These are women who believe that men have dominated western society throughout history and, as a result, women have been treated unfairly. The Women's Movement has worked for the equality of women in all aspects of life including equal rights, equal pay and equal job opportunities. Some of the changes that they have managed to achieve in the last 150 years have been the freedom to buy and sell land, the right to vote, the right to equal opportunities in employment and promotion and the right to ask for a divorce.

There are still some areas of life in which feminists believe women are still not given equality of treatment. For example, there are still more men than women in top management posts and it is said that women's sports receive brief and inadequate coverage in the media.

Do you think there are any other areas of inequality which need to be changed?

Heterosexual and homosexual

A fundamental part of our sexuality is our sex drive which informs us of our sexual needs and desires. While the majority of individuals feel a desire for the opposite sex it is now widely accepted that sexual desire does occur between those of the same sex . When men and women are attracted to each other they form **heterosexual** relationships. The legal age in Northern Ireland when a heterosexual may have full sexual relations (the **age of consent**) is 17. A **homosexual** relationship is when men are attracted to each other and women are attracted to each other. A female who has same-sex relationships is also called a **lesbian**. Those who have relationships with both the opposite sex and the same sex are **bisexual**.

Homosexuality between consenting males in private was decriminalised in Northern Ireland in 1982. The phrase 'consenting adults' was taken to mean over 21 years old but in 1994 the age of homosexual consent was lowered to 18 (Section 145 Criminal Justice and Public Order Act 1994).

Christian views of homosexuality cover a whole spectrum of opinions — from outright condemnation to full acceptance. Some Christians point out that the Bible clearly condemns homosexuality. For example, in Paul's letter to the Corinthian church he includes *"homosexual offenders"* among a list of the wicked who *"will not inherit the Kingdom of God."* (1 Corinthians 6: 9-10)

However, other Christians have tended to be less severe in their judgement of homosexuals stating that they understand and do not condemn feelings of homosexual love, although they still regard homosexual acts as sinful. For example, the **Catholic Church** teaches that homosexuals:

"do not choose their homosexual condition; for most of them it is a trial. They must be accepted with respect, compassion and sensitivity. Every sign of unjust discrimination in their regard should be avoided."

Catechism of Catholic Church 2358

Yet they also hold to their traditional view that:

"homosexual acts are intrinsically disordered".
Congregation of the Doctrine of the Faith, Persona Humana 8

Similarly, the **Methodist Church** believes:

"In keeping with the New Testament teaching, we are opposed to all debased forms of sexuality, whether homosexual or heterosexual, and we are opposed to homosexual behaviour. Nevertheless we plead for understanding and tolerance for those whose sexual orientation is towards those of their own sex. The Church should take a greater lead in the education of society, including Christians, regarding this issue, so that ignorance, prejudice and fear may disappear."

Methodist Belief

Questions

1 **Why is sexual stereotyping dangerous?**
2 **Do you think that there are differences in the way males and females of your age group are treated by:**
    - teachers
    - parents
    - other adults
    - each other?
3 **In your own words explain what feminism is and what it has achieved for women.**
4 **What is the current age of consent for:**
    a) homosexuals?
    b) heterosexuals?
    Do you think these ages should be lowered or made higher? Give reasons for your answer.
5 **Read 1 Corinthians 6: 9-10, 19-20. How might a Christian use these verses to object to homosexuality?**
6 **"It is a Christian's duty to show friendship to homosexuals and to treat them with equality and dignity." Do you agree or disagree with this statement? Give reasons for your answer.**

Sexual intercourse: a sacred act

Today we are able to talk about sex and sexual issues in a frank and open way. This is very different from previous generations when sex was a taboo subject and ignorance was rife. Our more open attitude has a lot to do with the public discussion of AIDS during the 1980s, when people realised that a lack of knowledge about sexual behaviour could be potentially deadly.

Not only is sex now freely talked about, but frequently we see sexual images on television and in advertising. When you look at a typical teenage magazine it is full of references to sex in the articles and letters it publishes. You may be left wondering if there is something wrong with you if you are not sexually active. A young person may feel under huge pressure to have sexual relationships because 'everyone else is doing it', but the truth may often be different.

Christians believe that sexual intercourse is a sacred act which should only take place in a committed marriage relationship. As such it is a wonderful gift from God:

[go to page 18]

"For the Christian sex is an essential part of human nature and there should be no sense of guilt if it is rightly used. The right physical use of sex is in marriage of a man and a woman. This is God's way by which children are born ... Sexual intercourse is also, in God's intention, a highly enjoyable thing. It is only wrong to use such instincts for purely selfish gratification, or in a completely irresponsible way."

The Presbyterian Church, Getting Married

Because sex is a sacred act there is no room for selfishness or for one person forcing their desires on the other. The full pleasure of sex can only be found when it is practised in a loving and caring way, when each partner respects the dignity of the other and is considerate of their needs. The **Methodist Church** emphasises this in a pamphlet on sexual issues called *Love is Enough*:

"The maximum enjoyment can only be experienced when both partners realise that sexual activity must be accompanied by understanding, affection and mutual trust."

Unfortunately, sex is not always carried out in a sacred way and the power of our sexual desires can lead to the act of sex being abused. Sex can be regarded as wrong when it is an act of pure selfishness, when it is not welcomed by one partner or when it leaves someone emotionally scarred. That is why Christians believe that sex is best reserved for marriage. In an intimate sexual relationship people are very close, at times vulnerable, and need to place a great deal of trust in each other. Over a period of time a couple will learn to understand each other and will want to please each other. Sexual relationships without commitment can leave those involved feeling hurt, used and emotionally scarred.

Another danger is the exploitation and abuse of our sexual appetites by advertisers who are trying to sell us anything from ice-cream to shampoo by using sexually suggestive images of men and, in particular, women. In these situations sexuality becomes part of the commodity which the advertiser is trying to sell. Some people feel that, as a result, sexuality is cheapened and we are encouraged to look at each other's bodies simply as objects. The Bible teaches that anything which demeans or harms the body is wrong:

"Don't you know that your body is the temple of the Holy Spirit, who lives in you and was given to you by God? You do not belong to yourselves but to God; he bought you for a price. So use your bodies for God's glory."

1 Corinthians 6: 19-20

Pre-marital sex

Abstaining from any sexual immorality (being sexually pure) is called **chastity**. Christians believe that all unmarried people should be chaste by avoiding sexual relationships. Here are some of the traditional reasons given why sex before marriage is not a good idea:

- There is a risk of pregnancy.
- There is a risk of sexually transmitted diseases.
- A sexual relationship requires commitment.
- To have sexual relationships with a number of people undermines the importance and sacredness of the act. For example, the Church of Ireland Standing Committee on Health has stated: *"We believe that human sexuality is a wonderful gift from God and, at a time in life when they are most aware of this gift, we would urge that young people question any behaviour that devalues this gift, or which hinders its fulfilment within the context of marriage."*

General Synod, 1992

- The Bible clearly teaches that sex should only take place between a man and woman in a marriage relationship:

"That is why a man leaves his father and mother and is united with his wife, and they become one."

Genesis 2: 24

The idea here of two becoming one is of a couple uniting in an intimate, sexual way.

If Christians believe that sex before marriage is wrong, the next question is 'How far should Christians go in a physical relationship with their boyfriend or girlfriend?' In her book *Going Out* Veronica Zundel lists some points to consider when making this decision:

◆ The decision should be mutual; no-one should be pressurised into doing things they don't feel happy about.
◆ The decision must be practical.
◆ The decision must take account of emotions.
◆ The decision must reflect the whole relationship. A relationship grows from distance to intimacy and the physical expression of it should not race ahead.

Singleness

It must always be remembered that while the majority of people in our society get married at some point in their lives there are still many who are single. This can be for a great variety of reasons — perhaps they have not found a suitable partner, their partner has died, they are divorced from their partner, or maybe they have made a promise to be single for religious reasons. In the Bible, St Paul commends the state of singleness:

"An unmarried man concerns himself with the Lord's work, because he is trying to please the Lord. But a married man concerns himself with worldly matters, because he wants to please his wife; and so he is pulled in two directions."
1 Corinthians 7: 32-33

Some religious orders ask their members to take vows of **celibacy**. This means they choose not to have sexual relations of any kind because they want to devote their lives to God and the service of others, as Christ did. They believe that the Church is their family and they don't want to be distracted from their duties by having a family of their own.

"Some profess virginity or consecrated celibacy which enables them to give themselves to God alone with an undivided heart in a remarkable manner".
The Catholic Congregation for the Doctrine of the Faith, Persona Humana 7

One Roman Catholic priest said:

"Celibacy is not an easy vow to live with. It requires you to be happy with yourself, knowing that you will have sexual thoughts but trusting that your faith will help you deal with these. Celibacy is not a miserable existence as some people might think. I lead a fulfilled and happy life and find I can offer my friendship to a greater number of people than would be possible in a committed relationship. The Bible offers encouragement for those who practice celibacy — Christ himself was celibate and St Paul said 'It is good to stay unmarried.' "

Of course, there are also those who are single because they are simply not 'going-out' with anyone. In a society where our sexual desires are constantly being teased and tempted, and where there is an expectation that people have partners, being single can be difficult. The **Presbyterian Church** recognises the difficulties of leading a single life but offers some practical advice and guidance:

"To channel energy and emotions along other lines is not easy, each individual has to seek the way and work out these matters personally. In this, as in all Christian obedience, prayer, faith, and discipline combined with practical ways of caring for others, will be of vital help."

It also reminds Presbyterians of the duty of the church to be inclusive of all its members no matter what their marital status:

" In the basic doctrine of the Body of Christ each member is a limb, making its own special contribution to the Body, and drawing its own sustenance from the Head, and in Him from each other. None may presume to be better than another nor attempt a role other than its own. In Colossians 2: 10 we find that there is fulfilment or completeness under the authority of Christ. While on earth He Himself chose the single life and denied Himself what home and family life brought to some with whom His relationship was so close."
Single Persons in Church and Community, 1989

Questions

1 a) What is celibacy?
   b) Give two reasons why a priest might argue that celibacy benefits him in his work.

2 a) What is chastity?
   b) What reasons might Christians give for being chaste until they are married?

3 In what ways might a single person 'channel their energy and emotions along other lines'? Give some practical suggestions.

4 a) Read 1 Corinthians 12: 12-27. What does Paul teach about the importance of all individuals in the church?
   b) In what ways could the Christian church help single people feel 'part of a whole body'?

'Honeymoon in Vegas' Nicholas Cage and Sarah Jessica Parker

MARRIAGE

If you have ever thought about the future there is a strong chance that you might have thought, "I wonder if I'll ever get married?" For many people marriage is the most important day of their lives. They plan a church wedding, invite all their friends and relatives and celebrate with a large reception in a hotel. This is still considered to be the norm but, increasingly, couples are choosing to do things differently. In the UK, marriage rates are declining and more couples are choosing to live together rather than marry. Northern Ireland's statistics are a good example of the general trend:

	1972	1991	1996
Marriages in Northern Ireland:	12,200	9,200	8,297

Another difference is that the number of people getting married in Registrars' offices rather than churches is increasing. In England a whole variety of places have been licensed for marriage ceremonies, from castles to football grounds.

However, marriage is not going to disappear. On the whole, people believe it should be highly valued. According to a recent survey carried out throughout Europe, 84% of people in Northern Ireland believed marriage to be still relevant.

WHY do PEOPLE get Married?

Marriage is the pinnacle of a loving relationship. To say publicly through the marriage vows "I will love you forever" is the ultimate declaration of devotion. Yet the motives which an individual may have for getting married usually go beyond a simple desire to say "I love you". Everyone has expectations of marriage, from their actual wedding day to the future they will have together, and these expectations will all be part of the reason why people decide to get married. The following statements give some examples of the reasons people give for wanting to get married.

JULIE

I can't wait until my wedding day. It'll be the function of the decade. The ceremony is being held in the quaintest church, and a hundred or so guests will be coming to the reception which will be the best bit, the part I've been looking forward to the most. I sometimes have to stop and pinch myself when I think about the whole thing, it seems that all my dreams will come true.

DECLAN

Sinead and I are absolutely crazy about each other. I adore her and just know she's the one for me.

Could it be you? Most people marry at some time in their lives.

TREVOR

I married Tina ten years ago when she got into trouble. I thought I was being a real romantic hero and proposed straight away. Luckily, things have worked out fine for us, but it could've easily gone wrong because, to be honest, I hadn't a clue about what getting married really involved. It changes your life.

PATRICIA

Getting married was the worst decision of my life. I remember before we tied the knot thinking that I simply couldn't live without Jim. The truth was that we couldn't spend five minutes together without nagging and fighting. Sometimes we had really major rows and I would get scared that I might lose him. So I suggested we get married, and he agreed. I thought we would grow into a dreamy, loving relationship in which we enjoyed every second of being together. It lasted two painful years.

Questions

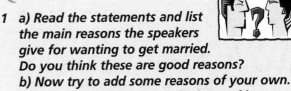

1 a) Read the statements and list the main reasons the speakers give for wanting to get married. Do you think these are good reasons?
   b) Now try to add some reasons of your own.
2 What expectations does Julie have of her wedding day? Do you think she is being realistic?
3 In your own words, describe what Patricia thought married life would be like. Do you share her impressions? Write down some of your ideas about what you expect married life to be like.

Discussion

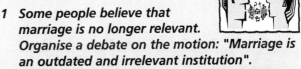

1 Some people believe that marriage is no longer relevant. Organise a debate on the motion: "Marriage is an outdated and irrelevant institution".
2 Design a questionnaire on marriage to survey the opinions in your class. Here are a few questions to get you started:
   - What age should you be allowed to marry?
   - In your opinion, how much money should be spent on a wedding?
   - How important is it for you to have a church wedding?

Christian Teaching on Marriage

"Man must not separate, then, what God has joined"
Mark 10: 9

Although Jesus goes on to mention the possibility of divorce in some circumstances, he states here what he sees as the ideal — a couple must commit themselves to a **life-long** relationship.

Read Ephesians 5: 25-33.

St Paul emphasises in this letter to the Christians at Ephesus that marriage is a relationship built on **love** and **respect.** The depth and sincerity of this love is so great that it can be compared to the love which Christ has for the church:

◆ He sacrificed his life for the church.
◆ He continually cares for the needs of the church
◆ He is united with the church so that Christ and the church are one.

So the partners in a marriage relationship should be united, care for the needs of one another and be prepared to put the other's life before their own.

What the Bible says

The Bible teaches that marriage is **sacred** and that God intended men and women to become one through marriage:

"Then the Lord God made the man fall into a deep sleep, and while he was sleeping, he took out one of the man's ribs and closed up the flesh. He formed a woman out of the rib and brought her to him. Then the man said, "At last, here is one of my own kind — bone taken from my bone, and flesh from my flesh. Woman is her name because she was taken out of man." That is why a man leaves his father and mother and is united with his wife, and they become one."
Genesis 2: 21-24

Marriage must also be a faithful relationship.

Read 2 Samuel 11-12: 25

In this story King David commits adultery with Bathsheba and has her husband killed. Despite his position of power and his previous favour with God, the prophet Nathan explains that David is not exempt from God's laws in which adultery is condemned (Exodus 20: 14).

When Jesus was asked about marriage and divorce he repeated the teaching from Genesis 2 but he also emphasised the **permanence** of marriage and the need for **fidelity** (faithfulness) by adding:

What the churches says

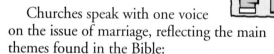

Churches speak with one voice on the issue of marriage, reflecting the main themes found in the Bible:

1 Marriage is **sacred.**
2 Marriage is **permanent**
3 Marriage is **exclusive**

Here is an example of each:

SACRED
"The intimate community of life and love which constitutes the married state has been established by the Creator and endowed by him with its own proper laws ... God himself is the author of marriage"
Roman Catholic Church, Gaudium et Spes 48.1

PERMANENT
"According to the teaching of Christ, marriage is a life-long union in body, mind and spirit, of one man and one woman. It is his will that in marriage the love of man and woman should be fulfilled in the wholeness of their life together, in mutual companionship, helpfulness and care. By the help of God this love grows and deepens with the years."
from the Methodist Marriage Service

EXCLUSIVE
"Marriage is a life-long partnership of man and wife, with absolute faithfulness the one to the other."
Getting Married, The Presbyterian Church

Preparation For Marriage

As we have discovered, marriage should not be taken lightly but, for Christians, it is a sacred and serious event. In order to make sure that a couple realise what marriage involves and to prepare them for life together, most churches hold **marriage preparation classes.**

The importance of marriage preparation is being increasingly emphasised as it is felt that proper preparation for marriage prevents the early breakdown of relationships.

A priest or minister will discuss the wedding arrangements with a couple, as well as offering advice and instruction on such issues as the purpose of marriage, sex, money, church life and personal relationships.

Here are some basic questions a couple may be asked to think about:
- Why are you getting married?
- Why do you want to be married in a church?
- Do you both want a family?
- How will you organise your money?

Activity

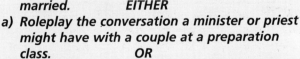

Think of other things a couple need to consider when getting married.   *EITHER*
a) *Roleplay the conversation a minister or priest might have with a couple at a preparation class.*   *OR*
b) *Write out the notes a minister or priest might use when preparing for a marriage preparation class. Here are a few headings to get you started.*
   - Regular church worship after marriage.
   - Responsibilities within marriage.
   - The need for faithfulness.

The Wedding Ceremony

Christians believe that marriage should take place in Church because it is not just a legal agreement but a sacred bond carried out before God.

Wedding ceremonies vary greatly from church to church but there are certain important features which most have in common.

Introduction and Declaration of Purpose

Generally there is a short sermon or homily in which the priest or minister speaks about the importance and purposes of marriage.

The Vows

These are required by law, although the wording may change from church to church. Here is one example:
" I (name) do take thee (name) to be my lawful wedded wife/husband, to have and to hold from this day forward; for better, for worse, for richer, for poorer, in sickness and in health, to love and to cherish, till death do us part."

Exchange of rings

Rings are exchanged at a marriage ceremony because they symbolise the promise of unending love and the exclusive commitment which each partner is making.

Warning

Minister quotes Jesus' words
"Man must not separate, then, what God has joined together" Mark 10: 9

Pronouncement

It is stated that the couple are now married

Signing of the register

This is a legal requirement in which a couple (and witnesses) sign a register and receive a marriage certificate. Many ordained priests and ministers are licensed Registrars and are authorised to issue marriage certificates. If they are not then a state Registrar must be present.

Questions

1 Below is an example of an order of service from a Church of Ireland wedding.
   a)   Do you think these hymns are appropriate for a wedding? Explain why.
   b)   Look up Psalm 67. Why do you think this particular Psalm was read?
   c)   Do you think the order of service could be improved in any way? What changes would you make to this ceremony and why?
2 Explain why couples exchange rings at a wedding ceremony.
3 In Christian marriage what do you think is meant by the phrase 'the two shall become one'?
4 a)   Why do Christians believe it is important for them to get married in church?
   b)   Do you think a minister or priest has the right to refuse to marry a couple who never attend church?
5 Show in detail how the Christian ceremony reflects Biblical teaching.

✝ ✝ ✝ *Order of Service* ✝ ✝ ✝

Trumpet Voluntary.........Jeremiah Clark

Hymn.......*Be still for the presence of the Lord*

Marriage Ceremony

Hymn.....*Tell out, my soul, the greatness of the Lord*

Collect.....................Psalm 67

The Address

The Acclamations

Prayers

Hymn................*Lord of all hopefulness*

Signing of the Register

Trumpet Tune...............Henry Purcell

Activity

In pairs try to make a list of other traditions which are associated with wedding services and ceremonies.

INTER-CHURCH MARRIAGE

This statue in Derry City symbolises two communities trying to reach out to each other and close the gaps of mistrust.

The phrase **inter-church marriage** simply refers to the marriage of couples from different Christian churches. In Northern Ireland when this involves a couple from both Protestant and Catholic backgrounds, it is often referred to as a **mixed marriage.**

In general there are few problems experienced by couples from different Protestant churches who want to get married. Those entering mixed marriages, however, can suffer difficulties in several ways. There may be strong disapproval of the marriage by one or both of the families of the couple, there may be problems finding a church to marry them and they could find it difficult to find a place to live where they will feel safe. So can mixed marriages work? The following two interviews tell the real stories of people who have experienced relationships in which the couple are from different traditions.

Interview 1

Jackie and Seamus met on holiday in Ibiza and are now engaged to be married. Jackie, a Methodist, was brought up in Co Down and Seamus, a Catholic, has lived all his life in Dublin. Seamus is hoping to find work as soon as possible in Belfast where they want to buy their first house. In an interview with the authors of this book Jackie talks about her attitude to mixed relationships:

Was the religion of your boyfriends ever an important issue to you?

No, I've never been worried about anyone's religion. I always see people as people. I take them for what they are.

What about your family? Were you ever wary of their opinion?

When I was 18, I started to go out with a Catholic boy in our class. Everyone liked him and none of us cared what church he went to. My parents liked him at the beginning but when they thought it was getting serious they advised both of us to finish the relationship, pointing out the problems we would have to face in the future. I was embarrassed about this in school when people found out.

What problems do you think your parents were talking about?

They thought it would be difficult to decide where to get married, where to live and, probably most important to them, what religion our children would be.

Do you think their concerns were realistic?

I thought they were being very sensible about the whole thing, but in some ways they took advantage of our naïvety and exaggerated the problems, considering that some of their friends were in mixed marriages and didn't have any problems. But I never told them about any boyfriends after that because I didn't want them to interfere. In some ways, however, I wanted to tell them what I was doing but couldn't.

So when you met your fiancé how did you feel about telling your family?

I was dreading it, but I knew they would not influence me this time. I was eight years older and felt I could make my own decisions.

That was three years ago; how have things changed since the first meeting?

My parents love Seamus and are delighted that I have chosen him to be my husband. Discussion of marriage has not been a problem as Seamus decided from the start that we would get married in my church and our children would be brought up in the Protestant tradition. This pleased my family. But I do understand the difficulties that other couples must have with this and I don't know if our relationship would have lasted if there had been opposition from both our families.

Interview 2

Catherine was born out of a mixed marriage thirty years ago. Here she talks about her experience of growing up in a family influenced by both Catholic and Protestant traditions.

"My parents were married thirty-five years ago. My father was a Presbyterian divorcee and my mother was from a very devout Roman Catholic background. Both their families disowned them when they married, so I grew up knowing nothing of my relatives. In fact the first I knew that I had a grandmother was when she was dying. I was fourteen. She asked to see Daddy before she died.

I was brought up as a Roman Catholic, but my mum always stressed that I should make up my own mind. I always had a deep respect for religion and had an enquiring mind. When I was sixteen I joined the Presbyterian church and stayed there ten years. I haven't been to church for a while but I'm thinking of going back to the Catholic Church. The truth is, I can see strengths and weaknesses in both systems without being blinded by prejudice. I believe my background has made me very open-minded but sometimes I have a bit of an identity crisis — I don't know where I belong."

Church teaching on inter-church marriage

It is important to note that no churches in Ireland try to prevent inter-church or mixed marriages from taking place, although they do warn that mixed marriages need to be entered with caution and couples should be aware of the difficulties which may arise. For example, what church will the couple get married in and attend when married? What are the attitudes of the couple's families to the marriage — are they likely to make things difficult? If there are any children, will they be baptised and, if so, in which church? Where will the children be educated — in a state school, a Catholic school, or an integrated school?

Activity

a **Imagine you are in a similar situation to Jackie and Seamus. In groups of four, roleplay the conversation they might have with Seamus' parents who are not happy with the proposed marriage.**
b **In groups read the following church statements on inter-church marriage. Each group should summarise the views of the different churches about:**
i) **the freedom of inter-church marriages to take place, and**
ii) **the issues which a couple should think carefully about before entering into an inter-church or mixed marriage.**

Methodist Church
"People should be free to marry whom they choose, worship where and how they choose, and bring up their children in the manner and denomination they consider best, without authoritarian pressure from any church or society ...
There should be freedom for inter-church (Protestant and Roman Catholic) marriages to be solemnised in either church in accordance with the wishes of those seeking marriage. Where joint pre-marriage courses are available, engaged couples are encouraged to attend."
Methodist Belief

Roman Catholic Church
The Roman Catholic code of Canon Law (1983) states that permission for a mixed marriage should only be granted if the following conditions are met:
1 The Catholic partner must try their best to make sure that all children are baptised and brought up in the Catholic faith.
2 The non-Catholic partner must be made aware of this duty.
3 Both partners must participate in a marriage preparation class.
In reality this means a Catholic must ask for a 'dispensation' to marry a non-Catholic if they wish the marriage to take place in a Roman Catholic Church, and a 'dispensation-from' form if in a Protestant church. However, this does not mean that the Roman Catholic Church is opposed to mixed marriages, but they do advise a couple to think twice — "Difference of confession between the

spouses does not constitute an insurmountable obstacle for marriage. But the difficulties of mixed marriages must not be underestimated ... Differences about faith and the very notion of marriage, but also different religious mentalities, can become sources of tension in marriage, especially as regards the education of children"

Catechism of the Catholic Church 1634

Presbyterian Church

"In marriage with a Roman Catholic, or in other circumstances where the partners do not share together in Church life and fellowship, they are handicapped by this and may be under continual strain in their relationships and family responsibilities. For this reason the Church cautions against entering such a partnership. Where this cannot be avoided, there is the greater need for faith and for Church fellowship to sustain and encourage both partners in Christian living."

Getting Married

Church of Ireland

The House of Bishops in 1975 approved of mixed marriages in either Roman Catholic or Church of Ireland churches as long as a minister is satisfied that the Roman Catholic partner will not prohibit the other partner "from exercising freely their responsibility in conscience regarding the baptism and upbringing of any children of the marriage".

Questions

1 What are the possible problems faced by a couple who enter a mixed marriage in Northern Ireland?
2 Do you think community relations in Northern Ireland would be improved if inter-church marriage were more common?
3 What might the advice of a priest or minister be for a couple contemplating an inter-church marriage?
4 In your opinion is life any harder for children of inter-church marriages than for other children?
5 What advantages and disadvantages do children have if their parents come from different church backgrounds?

DIVORCE & REMARRIAGE

Divorce is defined as a **legal process involving the civil authorities (the State) which ends in a declaration that a marriage is at an end.**

When people get married they think their love will last forever; they believe that marriage is for life. Yet in Northern Ireland it is estimated that 1 in 3 marriages end in separation or divorce. For example, in 1994 there were 2,303 divorce decrees.

Why do marriages run into trouble?

The number of divorces has increased dramatically over the last twenty years. It is never easy to give a single reason for a marriage ending, but there are some common pressures which couples find difficulty in coping with and can lead to a breakdown in the relationship. Here are some examples:

- disagreements over money
- infidelity (unfaithfulness)
- unemployment of one or both partners
- lack of communication
- different attitudes to sex
- high expectations
- health problems
- infertility
- pressures of caring for a child/children
- bereavement

In some circumstances one partner has sole responsibility for ending a marriage, but in the majority of cases it is impossible to identify clearly who is 'guilty' and who is 'innocent'.

The grounds for divorce in Northern Ireland

According to The Matrimonial Causes (Northern Ireland) Order 1978, to get a divorce in Northern Ireland a person has ... to satisfy the court that the marriage has irretrievably broken down and that one of the following grounds exists:

a) adultery by the other party;
b) behaviour which has made it unreasonable for the couple to live together;
c) desertion for two years;
d) the parties have lived apart for two years, and the other party consents to the divorce;
e) the parties have lived apart for five years.

Discussion

It is probable that in the future it will be necessary for a couple to undergo a period of counselling in an attempt to rescue their marriage before seeking a divorce. Do you think this is a good idea? Should couples be encouraged to try harder to make their marriage work?

The effects of divorce

1 On parents

Marital breakdown and divorce can cause much suffering. People often feel let down and fear what lies ahead. The emotional strain of beginning a new life is a cause of great stress for the divorcee and he or she can be faced with a whole set of practical problems. For example, he or she may never have had to deal with solicitors before or make and settle claims. There could also be the problem of looking after children as a single parent, which involves financial difficulties as well as making it hard to have a normal social life.

2 On children

Children of divorced parents can often suffer in the following ways:
◆ A child might feel torn between his or her parents.
◆ A child will have to live with one parent and the loss of day-to-day contact with the other parent may cause feelings similar to those experienced when suffering bereavement.
◆ All of these factors may result in personal stress symptoms, eg tearfulness, bedwetting, poor school work or bad behaviour.

Discussion

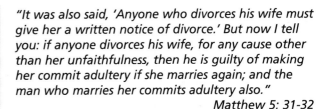

Statistics
* **The highest proportion of divorces takes place between couples who are married for approximately ten years and have small or young children.**
* **In 1993 it was estimated that 3,684 children in Northern Ireland were affected by divorce.**

In groups discuss the following questions:
1 **To what extent do you think children are affected by divorce?**
2 **Do you think that couples should ever stay together for the sake of their children?**
3 **In your opinion what could parents do to minimise the effects of divorce on their children?**

What the Bible says

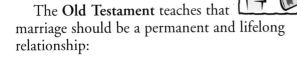

The **Old Testament** teaches that marriage should be a permanent and lifelong relationship:

"I hate divorce," says the Lord God of Israel, " I hate it when one of you does such a cruel thing to his wife. Make sure that you do not break your promise to be faithful to your wife."
Malachi 2: 16

Despite this the Old Testament mentions 'certificates of divorce' which a man could issue if:

"a woman ... becomes displeasing to him because he finds something indecent about her"
Deuteronomy 24: 1

Similarly, the **New Testament** states that divorce is wrong:

"Man must not separate, then, what God has joined together."
Mark 10: 9

"For married people I have a command which is not my own but the Lord's: a wife must not leave her husband; but if she does, she must remain single or else be reconciled to her husband; and a husband must not divorce his wife."
1 Corinthians 7: 10

However, Jesus' teaching in Matthew allows for one circumstance in which divorce may be permitted:

"It was also said, 'Anyone who divorces his wife must give her a written notice of divorce.' But now I tell you: if anyone divorces his wife, for any cause other than her unfaithfulness, then he is guilty of making her commit adultery if she marries again; and the man who marries her commits adultery also."
Matthew 5: 31-32

Some Christians argue that if Jesus showed compassion in this circumstance then there will be other, equally serious situations, in which divorce is permissible in his eyes. Do you think there are other serious circumstances when divorce should be allowed without question?

What the churches say

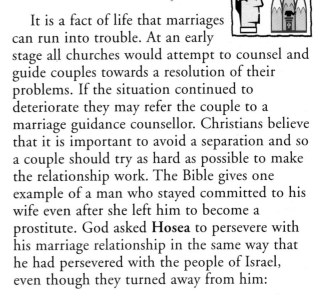

It is a fact of life that marriages can run into trouble. At an early stage all churches would attempt to counsel and guide couples towards a resolution of their problems. If the situation continued to deteriorate they may refer the couple to a marriage guidance counsellor. Christians believe that it is important to avoid a separation and so a couple should try as hard as possible to make the relationship work. The Bible gives one example of a man who stayed committed to his wife even after she left him to become a prostitute. God asked **Hosea** to persevere with his marriage relationship in the same way that he had persevered with the people of Israel, even though they turned away from him:

"How can I give you up Israel? How can I abandon you? ... My heart will not let me do it. My love for you is too strong."
Hosea 11: 8

But what if there is simply no way of mending the relationship and the couple wishes to get a divorce? Different denominations have different ways of dealing with this issue.

The Presbyterian Church, Methodist Church and Church of Ireland all accept civil divorce as an end to marriage. In general they permit the re-marriage of divorced persons, but only if the minister is willing to do so.

For example, the **Presbyterian Church** believes:

"At times human failure may even lead to the total breakdown of marriage, so that instead of a blessing it becomes a curse. Official separation and even divorce may then become the only course and one to be accepted by the Church ... It must be stressed that marriage is for life and all vows taken in marriage are "or better or for worse". Divorce can only be taken into the reckoning when absolutely all else fails. It can only be the last resort."

Getting Married

In the **Church of Ireland** the remarriage of divorced people has been permitted since the General Synod of 1995. However, it stresses the need for the consent of the clergyman and bishop.

Also, the **Methodist Church** states:

"The re-marriage of divorced persons in Methodist churches is permitted, upon due consideration of the circumstances, but no Methodist minister is required to officiate at such a marriage if he or she has a conscientious objection."

Methodist Belief

The **Roman Catholic Church** believes marriage is a sacrament and cannot be dissolved or ended. Even if a civil divorce is granted to a couple, the Church still believes that in the eyes of God they are still married and are not permitted to remarry.

"The matrimonial union of man and woman is indissoluble. God himself has determined it. 'What therefore God has joined together let no man put asunder.' (Matthew 19: 6)"

Catechism of the Catholic Church para 1614

"... there are some situations in which living together becomes practically impossible for a variety of reasons. In such cases, the Church permits the physical separation of the couple and their living apart ... In this difficult situation, the best solution would be, if possible, reconciliation. The Christian community is called to help these persons live out their situation in a Christian manner, and in fidelity to their marriage bond which remains indissoluble."

Familiaris Consortio 84

Catholics do believe that there are some situations in which a marriage may be **annulled**

(to declare that it never actually took place). For example, in the case of mental instability where one partner said the vows without understanding them, or immaturity, or if the marriage was never consummated (the couple never had sexual intercourse together).

Marriage guidance and counselling

A number of organisations exist to help couples who are experiencing marriage difficulties. Two of them are Relate and Accord.

relate

Relate Northern Ireland is part of Relate National. Its main objectives are:

1 To enhance the quality of couple and, thereby, parental and family relationships.
2 To help avoid unnecessary marriage and relationship breakdown.
3 To limit the damage which commonly accompanies poor relationships, separation and divorce, and increase the subsequent prospect of relationships succeeding.

Relate Northern Ireland offers the following services:

◆ Relationship counselling for couples and individuals with relationship problems.
◆ Psychosexual therapy.
◆ Family mediation (for couples who are separating or divorcing).
◆ RelateTeen (a counselling service for teenagers who are adversely affected by the break-up of their parents' relationship).
◆ Bookshop.
◆ Pre-marriage course and relationship programmes for schools.
◆ Client support course (for example 'Surviving the Break-up').
◆ Training for other professionals.

Things have changed a lot since this marriage guidance counselling session!

Catholic Marriage Counselling Service

Accord (previously Catholic Marriage Advisory Council) is a Christian organisation based on Catholic principles which offers counselling and mediation services to people of all religious, social and cultural backgrounds.

The services offered by Accord include:

◆ Marriage guidance counselling.
◆ Information on the natural method of family planning.
◆ Education service, eg, pre-marriage classes, sex-education information etc.

Questions

1 Find the correct definitions of the following words: infidelity; separation; desertion; sacrament; annulment; dissolution.
2 What opinions about divorce are contained in the Bible?
3 Explain why the Catholic Church is opposed to divorce.
4 Do you think churches are right to refuse to remarry a divorced person?
5 What problems may result from churches not accepting divorce?

Activity

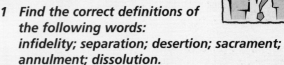

Arrange for a representative from Accord or Relate to visit your class and explain the work they do in more detail.

FAMILY PLANNING

'The Addams Family' Raul Julia and Anjelica Huston

PARENTHOOD AND FAMILY PLANNING

Parenting is a demanding and responsible job and a couple need to think carefully before having a family. There are the obvious issues of time and money to consider, as well as the effect on the couple's relationship, their plans for the future and the health of the mother.

Because of the responsibilities involved it is wise to plan for children; to decide how many to have and when. Family planning is possible by using either contraceptives or natural methods.

Discussion

In groups discuss:

1 *What are your impressions of being a parent? Would having a child make you feel differently about yourself? How would it affect the way you live or your plans for the future?*
2 *Make a list under each of the headings: 'The Joys of Parenthood' and 'The Demands of Parenthood'.*

Natural methods

The natural method of family planning works by a couple regulating their sexual activity to avoid intercourse on the days in a month when the women is fertile. This is the method of family planning advocated by the Roman Catholic Church, as they believe it is the only method where there is respect for the whole person.

Contraceptives

Contraceptives (the prevention of pregnancy by physical or chemical means) are not a modern invention. In ancient Egypt, tomb paintings show men wearing brightly coloured linen sheaths, and the Jewish Talmud advises the drinking of a 'cup of roots' as a contraceptive method.

Today the four most common types of contraception are the condom, the pill, the cap and the coil.

The reasons why a couple may want to use contraception, or natural methods of family planning may be:
— to prevent having children which they can't afford;
— to space their family;
— to avoid possible health risks which pregnancy brings a woman;
— they already have children and couldn't cope with any more.

Christians and contraception

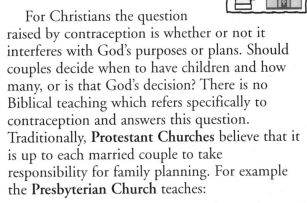

For Christians the question raised by contraception is whether or not it interferes with God's purposes or plans. Should couples decide when to have children and how many, or is that God's decision? There is no Biblical teaching which refers specifically to contraception and answers this question. Traditionally, **Protestant Churches** believe that it is up to each married couple to take responsibility for family planning. For example the **Presbyterian Church** teaches:

"In practice, Protestant Christians hold that it is not wrong to use various kinds of contraceptive devices, provided they are not used to evade having the size of family which the two partners together believe it is right for them to have and which they can support. Here too, young people before marriage would be well advised to consult a doctor. Alternatively, in many places there are excellent and wholly reliable family planning clinics, staffed largely by women doctors and nurses."
Getting Married

The **Methodist Church** sees a greater role for the local church by educating and counselling its married couples:

"The Church advocates responsible family planning within a marriage, with full provision of contraceptive services. The Church must also accept its responsibility to provide adequate counselling at all levels."
Methodist Belief

One Protestant church, the **Church of Ireland**, believes that it has a duty to advise young people, including those who are not married, about the benefits of contraception:

The condom (sheath, rubber)

Worn by a man, the condom provides a physical barrier which stops sperm from getting into the vagina. It also protects against the spread of sexually transmitted diseases.

The pill

The pill alters female hormones to prevent conception from taking place. It can have unpleasant side effects.

The cap or diaphragm

This is a barrier inserted by a woman into her vagina which prevents sperm from travelling through the cervix. After sexual intercourse the cap should be left in place for at least six hours.

The coil or inter-uterine device

This is inserted into the womb by a doctor. It is not known exactly how it works, but it either prevents a fertilised egg from attaching itself to the womb lining or the existence of this foreign body causes an inflammatory response which fights anything like bacteria, viruses or sperm.

These are the most popular types of contraception but there are many others available, including the male pill and the female condom.

"Family planning is the responsibility of married couples ... It would be mistaken to suggest that those involved in a sexual relationship outside marriage do not also have a serious responsibility with regard to both contraception and the reduction of risk in association with HIV/AIDS."
Standing Committee on Health, 1992

The **Roman Catholic Church**, however, is strongly opposed to all means of artificial contraception. It believes that all sexual intercourse must be open to the possibility of creating new life, as the unity of married love can never be compromised:

"So the Church, which is 'on the side of life', teaches that 'each and every marriage act must remain open to the transmission of life'. "

If a Catholic couple do wish to plan their family they must do so by using 'natural methods':

"For just reasons, spouses may wish to space the births of their children ... the methods of birth regulation based on self observation and the use of infertile periods, is in conformity with the objective criteria of morality."
Catechism of the Catholic Church 2366-2370

Questions

1 **What are the advantages and disadvantages of family planning?**
2 **Do you think that churches who agree with contraception should educate young people about the benefits of using it? Give reasons for your answer.**
3 **Explain how a Catholic who objects to using artificial contraception might still plan their family responsibly.**

Activity

Organise a TV style debate with representatives from two churches, a nurse from a family palnning clinic, a parent, a teacher and several teenagers to discuss the recent installation of a condom machine in the toilets of a local secondary school.

Responsible Parenting

If a couple does choose to have children then they must make sure that they look after the physical, emotional, intellectual and spiritual needs of each child in a caring and responsible way. It may seem obvious to say that parents must take care of their children but every year hundreds of children are neglected, injured or killed because of poor parenting. So just what is a responsible parent?

Being a responsible parent involves:

◆ providing for the material needs of a child and attending to his or her physical demands. The family home should be a place of comfort, warmth and happiness;
◆ giving love, care and time to a child;
◆ being responsible for the behaviour of your children and having the right to discipline them within reason;
◆ ensuring that your children go to school until they are at least 16;
◆ deciding which religion, if any, you want your children to be brought up in;
◆ not mistreating or harming a child through shaking, hitting or neglect;
◆ protecting your child from abuse. (Child abuse takes many forms – emotional, mental, physical and sexual);
◆ asking for help if there are problems (eg making sure an ill child is taken to a doctor).

Activity

'Childline' is an organisation set up to help children who are suffering from any kind of abuse or who feel they have no-one to turn to. Find out as much as you can about the organisation and design a poster advertising their work.

('Childline': 0800 1111)

Adoption and Fostering

Definitions

Adoption

Adoption describes the process by which a child is provided with a new family when living with his or her own family is not possible. The new parents become legally responsible for the child. The original parents no longer have any legal rights regarding the child; they are not allowed to see the child again or claim him or her back.

Fostering

Fostering involves taking care of a child for a temporary period of time without taking full legal responsibility. Children are often unable to live with their parents for a number of reasons and a good foster home may be the best alternative to staying at home.

Adoption

The number of babies being offered for adoption has decreased in recent years. This may be because abortion has become more acceptable or because there is less stigma attached to being a single mother.

Children are adopted through the **Adoption Service** or **Adoption Agencies**. These are organisations which are legally allowed to arrange adoptions by placing children in suitable families. However, only a court can make the arrangement legally binding. This is done by the court making an Adoption Order. This means a child becomes a full member of his/her adoptive family in the eyes of the law. The natural family have no longer any rights over the child.

So we can see how adoption is a serious issue. A couple need to think very carefully before either putting a child up for adoption or adopting a child themselves.

Giving a child up for adoption

A woman might want to give her child up for adoption for a variety of reasons:

- She has moral objections to abortion.
- A child may have a disability and the parents feel unable to cope.
- A baby may be born outside marriage and the mother may feel adoption is the best choice for the future.
- The mother may feel she is too young or too old to look after a child.
- The baby may be born as a result of rape.

However, reaching the decision to give your child up for adoption is never easy and those who take this option must realise that once a child is adopted the natural parents are no longer entitled to see him or her and cannot change their minds. They also play no part in choosing a family for the child. The adoption agency will respect their wishes regarding religious upbringing but stress that they always put the child's interests first when choosing a family. Finally, in years to come, a child may want to trace his or her natural parents (a person is legally allowed to do this when he or she is 18) so if a couple put their child up for adoption they must realise that one day their child may try to find them.

Adopting a child

In the majority of cases couples who adopt children do so because they are unable to have children themselves. Before being considered as prospective parents they must:

- have suitable accommodation;
- show general suitability to care for children and be prepared for some disruption to their way of life.

The adoptive parents need to be one hundred per cent certain that they will be able to cope with adopting a child. They need to be in good health and feel sure that they can cope with another family member. Sometimes there is a query about the physical or mental well-being of a baby or about the circumstances of their conception (eg babies born as a result of rape). Such difficulties are significant for the adoptive couple, especially when it comes to telling the child about his or her background.

British Labour MP Clare Short gave up her baby son for adoption. Many years later he traced his mother and they were reunited in 1996.

Benefits of adoption

Agencies, parents and adopters all have the child's best interests at heart when he or she is adopted. While living without one's natural parents is not ideal, it is hoped that those who adopt can provide a stable home where good care and attention are a priority and children can receive love and affection.

Fostering

Fostering is very different from adoption. Some people think that fostering can lead to adoption, but it is a mistake to think of fostering as a 'back door' to adoption. It is a service offered by a local authority to help families at times of stress. The main aim of fostering is to keep families together. The **National Foster Care Association** explains that:

"Foster care involves looking after someone else's child or teenager in your own home and working closely with the child's parents, with the help of the local authority or a voluntary organisation."

(Note: The National Foster Care Association is a charity working throughout the United Kingdom to promote and improve the service provided for children in foster care.)

Types of fostering

There are different types of fostering. Children can be fostered for days, weeks, months or even years.

1 Long-term fostering
Caring for a child for a period longer than six months. The child may eventually return home or become independent (usually at 18).

2 Respite fostering
Caring for a child for short periods to give the usual carers breathing space.
3 Bridge fostering
Carers offer support to help young people become independent.
4 Emergency fostering
Caring for a child overnight due to an unforeseen crisis.
5 Short-term fostering
Caring for a child for up to six months.
6 Pre-adoptive fostering
Caring for a new born baby for a few months.

As you can see, most children return home quite quickly but there will always be those for whom that is not a possibility. In these cases adoption may be the best option. The foster carer's job then involves helping the child to move on to an adoptive family.

Why are some children fostered?

1   The child's parents may be experiencing a family crisis and feel unable to cope. For example, one parent may be ill or suffering from bereavement.

2   If a child has been hurt, either physically, emotionally or sexually, it might be best for him or her to be removed from their home and placed with foster carers.

3   Some children have extreme behavioural problems and the parents need help to work out what to do next.

4   The family of a disabled child sometimes needs a break.

Rewards and challenges of fostering

Foster care brings both rewards and challenges. Imagine the achievement a carer feels when an unhappy toddler smiles for the first time or when they gain the respect of a sullen teenager. It can also be very satisfying for a carer to see a child and their parents happily reunited.

These rewards don't come easily and a carer must give one hundred per cent commitment and determination. Fostering can take a lot out of you physically and requires a great deal of patience. To be a good carer you must:

◆ be receptive to outside help as love is not enough to enable a person to look after someone else's children;
◆ take into account a child's history and feel able to deal with the whole picture;
◆ recognise tensions that will arise if you already have children of your own.

Christians, adoption and fostering

Adoption is seen as a natural practice in the Bible. If a child was left without parents, the extended family would take responsibility for them.

Read Esther 2: 5-7

Esther was a Jewish heroine who was adopted by her cousin Mordecai when her parents died. This difficult start in life did not hold Esther back as she went on to become Queen of Persia and rescued her people from their enemies.

The theme of adoption is used in the **New Testament** by Paul when he is talking about the relationship God has with Christians. On several occasions he refers to Christians becoming God's own children.

Christian churches have a history of involvement with adoption and fostering. The Church of Ireland and the Roman Catholic church both run adoption agencies. They do not have the power to finalise an adoption — this is a job for the courts — but the agencies match children with suitable families.

Interview

Teresa O'Hara (name changed) is a 72 year old grandmother. She grew up in Moira, Co Down but has lived in Glasgow for over fifty years. During that time she fostered over 200 children and adopted two girls. In an interview she described her experiences:

"Can you tell us what life was like as a foster parent?"

"I fostered children from 1960-1988 through a church adoption agency in Scotland. Its main work today is to help children trace their natural parents, but back then it was involved in fostering. The type of fostering I did is called 'pre-adoptive fostering'. I mainly fostered new-born babies who had been put up for adoption. Things were very different in those days. You fostered a baby for six weeks and then they were placed in an adoptive home. I remember they used to choose a couple to match a baby. They would try to find a baby boy who looked like the adoptive father or, if it was a girl, to look like the mother. It was done by eye colour — I always remember brown eyes were really scarce!"

"Did you ever meet any of the natural parents or the parents who adopted the children you fostered?"

"No. In those days everything was very private. The children couldn't find their natural parents so I never met them. It's all changed now. Last September I got a phone call from a man in Plymouth. He's 27 now. I'd fostered him when he was six days old and kept him for six months. He wanted to know if I knew anything about his real parents but I could tell him nothing. When I'd fostered a baby I would be in one room with the baby and the social worker would be in another with the parents. I wouldn't get the baby until they had gone."

"Was it difficult to give up the babies when it came time for them to be adopted?"

"Oh yes, it was a heart-breaking job but it was very rewarding. Recently I got another phone call from a young man who wanted to know if I'd fostered him. I told him I had and he was so grateful. He said his adoptive mother had told him about me and he hadn't believed her. I cried afterwards — its very emotional when the children contact you again."

"Did you always foster new-born babies?"

"At the start, yes, but during the last ten years of fostering there were fewer babies being put up for adoption. It was more pre-school children with problems who came to me to be fostered. I remember a toddler, Elizabeth, who stayed with my family for four years. She had behavioural problems. When she first arrived at our house she ran upstairs, lay down on the bed and cried. But everyone loved her. She was adopted by a lovely Christian family. It was their third adoption and this time they wanted to adopt a child with problems. They brought her back three times to visit and on her last visit I told the social worker that she'd settled well with them. After that they went to England to live."

"What about adoption yourself — did you adopt any of the children you fostered?"

"I did. I adopted two girls. My daughter Karen is 35 years old. She was going to be adopted by another couple and then the adoptive father was killed. The poor mother couldn't cope so Karen came back to me and I adopted her. I also fostered a Down's Syndrome baby. Her parents left her in the hospital when she was born. They couldn't come to terms with her disability and couldn't face bringing her home. I'd given birth to ten healthy children of my own and I wanted to give something back to the Lord for being so good to me. I fostered Sue for ten years and then I adopted her. I was 58 at the time — I thought I'd be too old but, thank God, it was allowed. Sue celebrated her 25th birthday last week".

Questions

1 **What is the difference between fostering and adoption?**
2 **Give three difficulties a family might encounter as a result of adopting a child. How might these be overcome?**
3 **Why do you think unmarried mothers today are less likely to give their babies up for adoption?**
4 **Explain how a child might benefit from being fostered.**
5 **What motivated Teresa to foster and adopt the number of children that she did? What rewards do you think she has gained from her experience?**

Activity

Invite a member of an adoption or fostering agency to speak about their work to your class.

CHRISTIAN VALUES IN THE HOME

Christian parents believe it is their duty to bring their children up in a Christian way. This can include making sure that a child is disciplined, knows right from wrong and is taught the importance of Christian values and worship. Parents can do this in various ways:

1 Prayer — Teaching the child how to pray, which may involve learning the Lord's Prayer together as a family, saying grace before family meals and praying for and with the child daily.

2 Example — Children learn by example; this can be bad example as well as good. It is up to the parents to set a Godly example for their children both in what they say and in what they do in their day-to-day lives.

3 Teaching the child — Christian parents are encouraged to teach their children the Christian faith. They might do this by reading together privately from the Bible or by taking them to church.

4 Baptism — In the Church of Ireland, Roman Catholic, Methodist and Presbyterian Churches, parents can choose to have their children baptised. When a baby is baptised it is welcomed into the family of the church. It is hoped that when the child is old enough to decide for him or herself that they will choose to remain in the Christian faith.

Activity

Look at these statements which summarise the baptismal vows of three churches. Read them and make a list of ways they suggest Christian parents can reflect Christian values to their children.

The **Roman Catholic Church** believes that parents are primarily responsible for the education of their children. This includes religious education. It is up to the parents to create a loving family atmosphere inspired by their love for God and each other. The local church is a source of help and support to the parent in this situation.

The **Presbyterian Church** holds that, as Christians, parents should bring up their children in the teaching of Christ's church. This involves bringing their children regularly to church worship, setting a good example for them and providing warm Christian fellowship in the home. As a result, their lives should mould together as a family, reflecting Christ's command to love one another as he has loved them.

Parents in the **Church of Ireland** are urged to bring up their children as Christians within the family of the Church. They should not only bring them to public worship but should help them in private prayer, teach them the Christian faith and encourage them to come in due course to Confirmation and Holy Communion.

How important is a happy family?

Christian's believe that the family is the backbone of society because the values and attitudes acquired there regarding tolerance, discipline and charity, are the very things needed in a well-ordered society. A family environment of learning and sharing will develop a sense of identity and belonging. This enables a person to have self-confidence and respect and means they will behave in a sensible and dignified way in society.

Questions

1   Is it important for children to grow up in a family which practises Christian values? Give reasons for your answer.
2   Give three examples of religious observance in the home of a Christian family.
3   Look at the following list and choose which activities would, in your opinion, be the five most important for bringing a child up in a Christian environment. Give reasons for your choices.

★ *Regularly attending Church services and Sunday School.*

★ *Encouraging children to join Christian youth groups, choirs, clubs and organisations eg Girls'/Boys' Brigade, Scouts or Brownies.*

★ *Showing a good parental example.*

★ *Allowing open discussion and encouraging the child to ask questions.*

★ *Praying together as a family.*

★ *Encouraging the child to be confirmed and take communion.*

★ *Opening the family home as a place of hospitality.*

★ *Celebrating the true meaning of Christian festivals.*

★ *Giving support to others in the church, for example, the elderly.*

Discipline

Some people believe that many of the problems in society today are caused by parents not disciplining their children. One reason given is that many parents are simply unable to spend as much time with *their* children as their parents spent with them and this lack of time can cause problems. What other factors do you think can cause poor discipline?

How parents should discipline their children is a difficult issue. In 1989 as many as 91% of parents admitted that they smacked their children (*The Daily Telegraph* 10 August 1989). Many parents would say that they smack toddlers more than their older children because infants don't understand words or reasoning. They argue that young children respond more to hugs and smacks and have at times to be physically removed from a situation which presents a danger — for example, crawling towards a hot fireplace.

Discussion

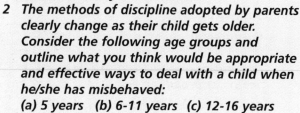

1 **What methods of discipline, other than smacking, can be used effectively with infants?**

2 **The methods of discipline adopted by parents clearly change as their child gets older. Consider the following age groups and outline what you think would be appropriate and effective ways to deal with a child when he/she has misbehaved:**
(a) 5 years   (b) 6-11 years   (c) 12-16 years

Questions

Read the Case Study below and then answer these questions.

1 **Do you think Ken and Audrey were good parents to Richard? How could they have done better?**
2 **Do you think Richard got too much freedom and not enough discipline? In your opinion, how much freedom should a teenager be allowed?**
3 **Name three groups of people who you think shared the responsibility for the moral development of Richard. Give reasons for your answer.**
4 **What influence for good can a stable family background have?**
5 **How important is the preservation of a happy home life in our society today?**

Case Study
What did they do wrong?

Ken and Audrey are examples of Christian parents who have tried to raise a stable, happy family, but failed. Their son, Richard, is on remand for joy-riding and burglary.

Audrey insists that Richard was a perfectly normal teenager. He went to Youth Centres, played sport and was a promising pupil at school and had chosen his GCSE subjects carefully. The family had always had firm rules on manners and behaviour, although Richard was never smacked or hit when he disobeyed them. As they thought they could trust him, Ken and Audrey allowed Richard to stay out as late as he wished at the week-ends. Ken and Audrey were horrified when they first got a letter home from school outlining how Richard had been rude to one of his teachers. That's when the trouble began.

Richard started to stay away from school,

claiming to be sick. He lost all interest in gaining good GCSE grades and would go out every night when he seemed to come to life. He took to vandalism and stealing cars and has been in and out of prison ever since.

"Maybe I should have been more strict with Richard when he was growing up," Ken remarked. *"But to tell you the truth I don't think we made many mistakes. What else could we have done? Locking him in his room and stopping his pocket money wouldn't have made any difference. Mind you, I still blame myself."*

"These last few years have been the worst," Audrey added. *"Ken has been up and down to that police station trying to sort things out. We've had social workers, probation officers — everyone on our backs. My head's turned! Maybe we should have hit him when he was younger? I don't know."*

What the Bible says

In the Bible there are many references to how people should behave in families. Both parents and children have duties towards one another.

In the **Old Testament** children are urged to:

"Honour your father and your mother."

Exodus 20: 12

With this comes certain expectations and responsibilities. Jewish parents were expected to teach the commandments to their children (Deuteronomy 6: 4-9) and were granted the responsibility of disciplining their young:

"If you don't punish your son, you don't love him. If you do love him you will correct him."

Proverbs 13: 24

"Don't hesitate to discipline a child. A good spanking won't kill him. As a matter of fact, it may save his life."

Proverbs 23: 13

Today there are parents who refuse to smack their children at all and believe that discipline should be about rewarding correct behaviour rather than punishing wrong behaviour.

It should be noted that Jesus showed a concern for the welfare of children when the disciples had lost patience with them:

"Let the children come to me, and do not stop them, because the Kingdom of God belongs to such as these."

Mark 10: 14

One of the most famous passages concerning parents and children is found in Paul's letter to the Ephesians, where Paul explains that a parent-child relationship should be built on respect:

"Children, it is your Christian duty to obey your parents, for this is the right thing to do. 'Respect your father and mother' is the first commandment that has a promise added: 'so that all may go well with you, and you may live a long time in the land.' Parents, do not treat your children in such a way as to make them angry. Instead, bring them up with Christian discipline and instruction."

Ephesians 6: 1-4

In Biblical times a great emphasis was put on the extended family and this would have involved caring for those relatives who were unable to care for themselves. We see this theme running through the entire Bible. In the Book of Proverbs God's people are advised that when your mother is old you should *'show her your appreciation'* (Proverbs 23: 22). This is underlined in the New Testament:

"But if anyone does not take care of his relatives, especially the members of his own family, he has denied the faith and is worse than an unbeliever."

1 Timothy 5: 8

Questions

1 **Paul taught that children should honour their parents and that parents should not provoke their children to anger. In what practical ways today could:**
   a) children honour their parents?
   b) parents respect their children?
2 **Read Colossians 3: 20-21. What reasons does Paul give for showing respect to your family members?**

Activity

a **In groups, design a Family Charter. Write a list of rules and conditions for both parents and children to keep. It must have the potential to make the family home a happier place to live in, eg "Don't expect perfection from other family members until you are able to offer it yourself".**
b **Organise a debate on the motion: "This House believes that you should never smack a child."**

ONe Parent FaMiLieS

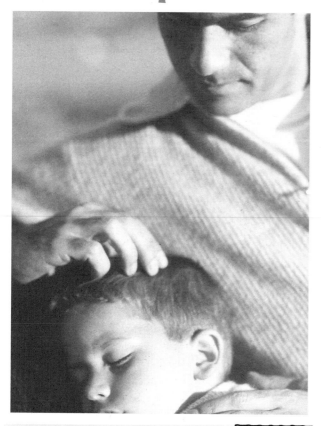

Activity

Write down the number of children in your family. Now try to remember how many were in your parents' families and then your grandparents' families. Do you notice a trend in your class? If so, why do you think this is the case?

Families have become smaller in recent generations because couples are having fewer children and only parents and children tend to share the same house. In the past many families were more frequently **extended**. A family can be described as being extended when it includes aunts, uncles, grandparents and cousins. A more typical image of a family probably consists of a husband, wife, and two children. This is known as a **nuclear** family. However, in our modern society families come in many shapes and sizes and there is no such thing as a typical family.

One type of family which is on the increase is the **single-parent** family. Children may be brought up by only one parent due to a bereavement, divorce, separation or perhaps because of a mother's decision not to marry or stay with the father of the child.

One young woman, **Louise**, from **South Belfast**, made this very decision:

"I was 19 when I had Orla. I was going with this fella at the time for a few months but it wasn't really serious. We had a laugh, went clubbing at the weekend, out with a crowd of mates — you know the sort of think. I was on the Pill but sometimes I was careless about taking it. I've certainly learnt from my mistakes! I near died when I missed my period. I had to buy one of those pregnancy tests. They're not cheap, y'know! Mind you, that's been the least of my money problems. It's so expensive bringing up a child — especially on your own. He didn't want to know. He thought I'd have an abortion but I'm dead against that. I haven't seen him since. My mum's been great — she looks after Orla at the weekends so I can still get out and about and have a break. During the week I haven't a minute to myself. I'm up at 6:30 am to get Orla ready for the childminder; then its straight to work and then back at 6:00 pm to collect her. Then I've to get us our teas, get her sorted for bed and by that time I'm wrecked. She's getting really cheeky too. I could do with someone else round the house to sort her out!"

Another man, **David**, from **Lisburn**, describes his life as a single parent:

"When Lily died I was devastated! It was so sudden. I was working for the council at the time. The children were old enough. Jennifer had just started Queen's University and John was in his last year at school. Jennifer got a grant so that was all right. I couldn't have afforded it otherwise. I was very lonely. Lily and I had been great for each other. The children felt lost without her as well. They started to treat the house more like a hotel. In the end my sister came round once a week to help with the chores. That was six years ago. Things have changed a lot since then and we feel more like a family now but those first few years were difficult."

Questions

1 **Read the experiences of Louise and David and make a list of the shared characteristics common to one-parent families.**
2 **In what ways are their experiences different?**
3 **Children from one-parent families often have to take on responsibilities at an earlier age. What might some of these be?**

Advantages and disadvantages of one-parent families

Being a single parent is not an easy task, particularly if the situation is caused by divorce or bereavement. For many people there is a big

adjustment to make in their lives when they find themselves being the only parent. Faced with the prospect of having to hold down a job and do everything else as well, many people simply feel that they are unable to cope. Some single parents find they have to work part-time, or else leave work altogether in order to look after the children. It can be a difficult for a parent to be constantly trying to find a baby-sitter and many people simply cannot afford one. Children are usually sent out to relatives and friends and this can lead to instability. If a parent does leave work, loss of adult company and conversation can lead to depression.

Lack of money does not ease the situation. A parent may feel they have let their children down if they cannot afford the same treats, like school trips, that other children are receiving. Young children in particular often do not appreciate money problems and this can result in temper tantrums. Unless you have close friends or relatives to turn to, it can be lonely having to bear all these worries on your own.

On the other hand, being part of a one parent family can have its advantages. Often there is a greater sense of closeness between the parent and the children, particularly if the parent does not work full-time and is there when the children get home from school. The children may show greater respect for their parent because they realise the situation is not easy and they are often more sensitive to the needs of other people outside the home. Sharing household chores and learning to look after themselves leads children to be more mature than is expected of them.

What the Bible says

In both the **Old** and **New** Testaments a special place is given to one-parent families. An example of such a family is found in the book of Ruth:

"Elimelech died, and Naomi was left alone with her two sons."

Ruth 1: 3

This type of situation was often unavoidable and the Bible teaches that God:

"cares for orphans and protects widows."

Psalm 68: 5

If a widow was ill-treated it was regarded as a serious offence:

"Do not ill-treat any widow or orphan. If you do, I, the Lord, will answer them when they cry out to me for help."

Exodus 22: 22-23

Jewish culture placed a great emphasis on family life so, when a woman was widowed, it was up to her family or the religious community to ensure her needs were met. In Acts 6 there is also evidence in the early Christian Church of daily distribution of funds being available for widows. But this was not solely the responsibility of the church. In 1 Timothy 5: 3-4 and 16 we read:

"Show respect for widows who really are all alone. But if a widow has children or grandchildren, they should learn first to carry out their religious duties towards their own family and in this way repay their parents and grandparents, because this is what pleases God ...
"But if any Christian woman has widows in her family, she must take care of them and not put the burden on the church, so that it may take care of widows who are all alone."

How can the church help?

Apart from giving financial help, 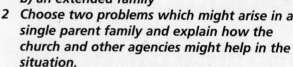 there are many ways in which the Church can ease the burden for single-parent families. In some churches, for example the Presbyterian Church, there is an elder appointed to look after the congregation living in a certain area. Through regular visitation an elder could help with practical matters such as small household tasks, gardening, transport as well as discussing any problems and offering a concerned and attentive ear. Of course, you don't have to hold an office of authority in a church in order to help those in need. Many churches have members who like to show their faith in a practical way. Some volunteer to help run a crèche or a 'mother and toddlers' group. Others help out with babysitting on a rota basis. Members of a congregation come from all walks of life, so if there is a financial advisor in the congregation they might hold an evening where

advice about budgeting can be given. Support like this from the church can be comforting and is often invaluable to the single-parent family.

Questions

1 Give a definition of:
   a) a nuclear family
   b) an extended family
2 Choose two problems which might arise in a single parent family and explain how the church and other agencies might help in the situation.
3 Do you think the Government gives enough support to single parent families?
4 How might Biblical teaching encourage the single parent?

Activity

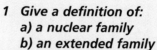

Find out all you can about organisations which help single-parent families eg St Vincent de Paul or Gingerbread.

'Immediate Family' Kevin Dillon

CARING AND RESPECT FOR LIFE

Christians believe that all life should be valued and respected. This is often summed up by the phrase: "Life is sacred from the womb to the tomb". In this unit we will explore how a respect for life influences Christians in their attitudes towards various groups in society such as the elderly and the marginalised. You will be faced with the dilemmas and feelings of those people who have struggled with questions such as what to do with an unwanted pregnancy or how best to alleviate the suffering of a loved one facing a painful death. It is hoped that you will begin to form your own opinions on these issues and deal with them in a sensitive and informed way.

Care of the Elderly

Many people look forward to their old age as a time when they can retire from work and enjoy being with their families. The more adventurous may go travelling or start new hobbies. The majority of old people live independent and interesting lives and cope with the ups and downs of daily living. However, old age does bring with it problems and extra help or assistance may be needed. Some of the difficulties which older people can experience include: loneliness, poverty, housing problems, illness, disability, bereavement and vulnerability.

Income

At their retirement most people experience a drop in their income and a change in lifestyle because their pension is significantly less than the wages they received previously. There are those who will receive additional money from a private pension scheme (money which they have saved during their working lives) but the majority of people are dependent on state pensions and benefits.

Activity

a   **In pairs try to make a list of some everyday examples of difficulties which an elderly person might face.**

b Find out what is the basic state pension in the UK for a single man more than 65 and a single woman more than 60. Make a list of all the types of bills and expense which would come out of a person's pension. How much would be left for spending money?

Housing

An elderly person's quality of life can be greatly influenced by their housing condition. It may be that a house has no central heating or is too large to maintain, or the elderly person becomes ill and cannot do basic housekeeping tasks. The results are often discomfort, cold, lack of security and restricted mobility.

On the other hand, elderly people who live in good accommodation which matches their needs and abilities can enjoy a high quality of life. Some initiatives which attempt to meet the housing needs of old people are:

Fold Housing

This is a small estate or community of pensioners' apartments or bungalows, like the one above, supervised by a warden and with access to twenty-four hour emergency help.

Community Care

This is a government policy which attempts to combine the services and care provided by local health authorities, families and voluntary groups to enable elderly people to carry on living in their own homes as long as possible.

Residential Homes

These are for people who are generally able to take care of themselves but who are unable to cope with living at home.

Nursing Homes

These are for people who need a lot of nursing care because they are ill, unable to walk, incontinent or unable to feed themselves.

Health

Although people are living longer because they are healthier, old age inevitably means a deteriorating state of health. This does not mean that all old people are sick. In fact the majority of old people remain fit and healthy to enjoy a full life, but there are some common health problems which people experience as they grow old. For example, loss of eyesight (97% of those over 65 wear glasses), loss of hearing, circulation problems, arthritis and problems of mobility.

Depression can also be a problem faced by old people. This can be caused by feelings of loneliness or worthlessness. For many people their job gives them a sense of purpose and belonging. When that is taken away from them they can feel they are no longer important or valued. This is made worse if an elderly person doesn't have the physical health to do the things they want.

Discussion

In pairs discuss your ideas of what a typical old person is like.

A common view of old people in our society is that they are 'past it' and no longer have anything valuable to contribute. Indeed they are often considered to be a burden to others. Unfortunately these ideas are reinforced by television, advertising and some employers who all make us believe that a fulfilling and successful life comes only to those who are young, healthy and good-looking. When people are discriminated against simply because they are old it is called **ageism.**

Not only are the elderly losing the respect once given to them by society, but they are also more vulnerable than ever before to criminals and attackers. They are seen as soft targets by those who wish to trick them out of their money, steal from them or even physically abuse them.

There are plenty of old people who do not fit into the stereotyped picture of what it means to be old. Many of them are active, valuable to the community and proud of their individuality. More old people could be helped to be like this if opportunities were offered to them which would use their skills and talents, as well as providing them with a sense of value to the society in which they live. Can you think of some ways old people could contribute to the community in which they live?

Charities for the elderly

There are many organisations which exist in order to help the elderly. Two of the largest charities are **Help the Aged** and **Age Concern**.

The services provided by these charities include:
◆ information publications (eg *Winter Warmth Guide*, or *Your Savings in Retirement*)
◆ operating advice telephone lines
◆ providing library facilities
◆ improving living conditions
◆ providing community transport
◆ running special housing facilities

What the Bible says

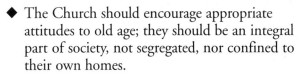

The Bible teaches that Christians should "Love your neighbour", (Luke 10: 27) and, of course, this includes the old. There are also a few references to caring for the elderly in particular.

The Old Testament includes the commandment:

"Respect your father and your mother, so that you may live a long time in the land that I am giving you."

Exodus 20: 12

and also states:

"Show respect for old people and honour them."

Leviticus 19: 32

"Listen to your father; without him you would not exist. When your mother is old, show her your appreciation."

Proverbs 23: 22

Respect from younger people for their elders is also seen in Job 32: 4:

"Because Elihu was the youngest one there, he had waited until everyone finished speaking."

The **New Testament** teaches that:

"If a widow has children or grandchildren, they should learn first to carry out their religious duties towards their own family and in this way repay their parents and grandparents, because that is what pleases God ... If anyone does not take care of his relatives, especially the members of his own family, he has denied the faith and is worse than an unbeliever."

1 Timothy 5: 4, 8

Jesus made sure that his mother Mary would be cared for as she got older and when he would not be there to look after her:

"Standing close to Jesus' cross were his mother, his mother's sister, Mary the wife of Clopas, and Mary Magdalene. Jesus saw his mother and the disciple he loved standing there; so he said to his mother, 'He is your son'. Then he said to the disciple, 'She is your mother'. From that time, the disciple took her to live in his home."

John 19: 25-27

What the churches say

Among their recommendations for supporting the elderly, **Methodists** and **Presbyterians** believe:

◆ The Church should encourage appropriate attitudes to old age; they should be an integral part of society, not segregated, nor confined to their own homes.
◆ Greater use should be made of the time and skills of recently retired members.
◆ Church members should provide the following types of support to old people: visiting, relief of relatives' strain, transport, social events and catering for their spiritual needs.
◆ Church members who are involved in the caring professions should provide some education and training for volunteers.
(Methodist Church in Ireland, *Occasional Papers Series* Vol 1, No 1, 1983/84 and *Senior Citizens Policy Document* report to the Presbyterian General Assembly)

Similarly the **Roman Catholic Church** believes:

"The fourth commandment reminds grown children of their responsibilities toward their parents. As much as they can, they must give them material and moral support in old age and in times of illness, loneliness or distress."

Catechism of the Catholic Church para 2218

Questions

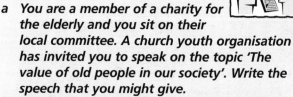

1 Explain 'ageism' and give some examples of occasions when people might be 'ageist'.
2 In what ways do charities for the elderly try to help old people?
3 In what particular ways do you think a church could care for the spiritual needs of an older person?

Discussion

"When a person reaches 65 they should realise they're over the hill and step aside to allow young people to take over." Do you agree or disagree? Give reasons.

Activity

a You are a member of a charity for the elderly and you sit on their local committee. A church youth organisation has invited you to speak on the topic 'The value of old people in our society'. Write the speech that you might give.
b Read the account below. What do you think will happen? In groups roleplay the family conversation.

What will we do about Granny?

Tim and Lorraine Anderson have been married for nineteen years. Tim is a successful businessman and Lorraine works part-time as a local hairdresser three days a week. They have three children, Andrew who is fifteen and studying for his GCSE's, Jenny an independent eleven year-old who has just started secondary school, and Michael aged seven who is still spoiled by his granny. Tim's mother, Joyce, is 82 and has been living on her own four miles outside town ever since her husband Bill died.

Earlier this year Joyce had a mild stroke and has found it difficult to make a full recovery. Last week she fell badly in the bathroom and spent a few days in hospital. Just last night Tim called in to find Joyce had gone to bed leaving on the electric fire in the living room. Tim has decided enough is enough and he wants his mother to move in with his family where they can keep an eye on her.

The Andersons have a four-bedroom house and Tim reckons the two boys could share a bedroom to make space for Joyce. He has mentioned it to his wife who feels uncomfortable with the idea but also recognises there are few alternatives. Tonight after dinner they are going to discuss the matter with the children.

Care of Marginalised People

Definitions

Prejudice

A negative view of someone based on an unfounded or unreasonable opinion, eg
"I don't like young people as they tend to be rude, noisy and don't appreciate anything you do for them".

Stereotyping

The assumption that a person shares all, usually negative, characteristics of a group to which it is assumed they belong, eg
"He must be lazy because he's from Armagh. All men from Armagh are lazy".

Discrimination

To act unfairly towards a person or to exclude someone from equal treatment, usually as a result of a prejudiced attitude, eg
"Women are only allowed to play golf on this course on Wednesday afternoons."

Here are some examples of people considered to be marginalised in our society:

◆ drug addicts
◆ gambling addicts
◆ alcoholics
◆ AIDS victims
◆ homeless people
◆ travelling (itinerant) people
◆ the mentally and physically disabled
◆ criminals and prisoners

A **marginalised** person is someone who is not given a full place in society. Many find themselves marginalised because of who they are, what they do or what people perceive them to be. They can be considered by the majority in society to be *different, unpleasant* or even *undesirable*. These judgements are often based on **prejudice** and **stereotypes** rather than a real understanding of the marginalised person's situation.

Unfortunately, it is often the case that marginalised people are not just disliked but they are deliberately over-looked, mistreated or exploited. When prejudice shows itself in action it is called **discrimination.**

Although we may sympathise with marginalised people, many of us have grown up with the attitude that "It's not my problem" or "They must deserve it", and we never examine the important question of how to change their condition as marginalised people. In some cases government or council action is necessary to help marginalised people, but the most significant changes which are needed are in the attitudes and the actions of individuals within society.

It is not always possible to pinpoint the reasons why people are marginalised but once a person or a group of people becomes marginalised it can be very difficult to break the cycle of disadvantage. For example, if a young person were to become homeless they could not claim any welfare benefits because they have no fixed address. If they have no money and no place to live it is almost impossible to get or hold down a job. Because they can't earn money they will never be able to afford any accommodation ...

Look at the following case studies and answer the questions which follow.

Case Study 1: Homelessness

Joe lived in a graveyard before being helped by Simon, a charity for homeless people. In common with many homeless people, he had no stable family life, and grew up living in care and with various foster parents. Here is his story:

"I was very lucky last Christmas. What with living in the graveyard, things hadn't been very good before Christmas. By November I couldn't stick the cold anymore and, hearing Simon helped, I came to their door. The warmth and shelter were great and very soon I got caught up in the plans for Christmas. I helped with the tree and putting up the decorations. I got the first Christmas card that I can remember from the Simon staff. We all got presents as well from the staff. I told them I liked drawing so I got sketch pads and paints. Most people got clothes. I've been with Simon almost a year now and I think I've gained enough confidence to start a home of my own."

Case Study 2: Alcoholism

Robert woke up to find himself lying in a neighbour's garden. He hadn't quite made it home yet — just as well, as his wife would only scream at him for spending his wages on drink. He had a thumping hangover but still needed another drink ... just one more, then he'd stop. Robert checked his coat — no money, just an empty bottle of whisky. He caught sight of his   unshaven reflection in the window of a parked car; he looked ten years older than he was. A neighbour saw him and crossed the road to avoid him. Robert felt ashamed. He couldn't change, he thought, it was too late for him ...

Case Study 3: Travellers

Frances was brought up as a traveller. Now she has her own family and they too are used to life on the road. Living on the fringe of society isn't easy. People are always pointing the finger at them, pressurising the council to move them on, and making them feel worthless.

Frances thinks that she deserves access to good sites with basic amenities. She worries about the health of her family and, like all parents she wants a good education for her children. She herself is illiterate and has never been able to fill in an application form for a job. She says: "It's not that I'm lazy, although that's what people think about us". When the children go to school they get bullied for being different and, as a result, often play truant. Frances is disappointed that things still haven't changed since she was a girl, "Now we're about to enter the twenty-first century. Surely things will get better," she says.

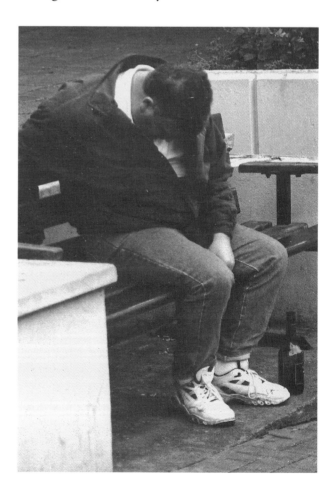

Questions

1 How had Joe become marginalised?
2 Explain what help Joe needed to make him feel he could be independent and part of society again.
3 What was the affect of Robert's alcoholism on his family and friends?
4 If you were to see someone like Robert in the street what would your attitude be towards him? Would you offer help?
5 Imagine you and your family are travellers and you have recently set up camp in an unwelcoming town. You are fourteen years old and have joined a local secondary school. Write a diary entry for two consecutive days describing your difficulties.
6 What do you think a Christian's attitude should be to travelling people? How could they help in a practical way?

Activity

a Research and write a project on the treatment of one marginalised group in our society. For example, examine how people's attitudes to disabled people can be marginalising.
b Organise a speaker from a charity that works with marginalised people to visit your class and talk about the people that they work with and how they try to help.

What the Bible says

The Bible is very clear in its teaching about people in society who are considered to be weak, powerless or outcasts.

In the **Old Testament** there is a fundamental recognition that all human beings are valued by God because they are made in his image:

"So God created human beings, making them to be like himself"

Genesis 1: 27

There are also many references to the need for **social justice**, which means the fair and proper treatment of all people in society. Here are just two examples:

"You are doomed, you that twist justice and cheat people out of their rights."

Amos 5: 7

"In the houses of evil men are treasures which they got dishonestly. They use false measures, a thing that I hate. How can I forgive men who use false scales and weights? Your rich men exploit the poor and all of you are liars. So I have already begun your ruin and destruction because of your sins."

Micah 6: 10-13

In the **New Testament** we can see in the example of Jesus someone who was concerned with injustice and poverty:

"Why should God reward you if you love only the people who love you? Even the tax collectors do that! And if you speak only to your friends, have you done anything out of the ordinary? Even the pagans do that! You must be perfect — just as your Father in heaven is perfect!"

Matthew 5: 46-48

"Then Jesus said to his host, 'When you give a lunch or a dinner, do not invite your friends or your brothers or your rich neighbours — for they will invite you back, and in this way you will be paid for what you did. When you give a feast, invite the poor, the crippled, the lame and the blind; and you will be blessed, because they are not able to pay you back. God will repay you when the good people rise from death.'"

Luke 14: 12-14

"Do for others just what you would want them to do for you."

Luke 6: 31

Other references to look-up:
Jewish law:
Deuteronomy 25: 15-16
The parable of the Good Samaritan:
Luke 10: 25-37
Jesus and Zacchaeus:
Luke 19: 1-10
The parable of the sheep and the goats:
Matthew 25: 31-46
The man with a dreaded skin disease:
Luke 5: 12-14

What the churches say

There is a long history of Christian involvement with marginalised people. All churches recognise the value of every individual and the responsibility of Christians to help others.

A report, given to the Methodist Conference in 1995, stated:

"We call on Methodists in Northern Ireland to overcome age-old stereotypes and prejudices and to actively pursue levels of acceptance and tolerance. Let us leave no stone unturned to see that no group nor individual experiences discrimination."

Report on Pluralism

Here are just a few examples, past and present, of how churches and individuals have attempted to follow Christ's teaching and example to love others.

Liberation Theology

Liberation Theology is a movement which began in Third World countries. It identifies the peoples of the Third World as marginalised and holds that there is a Christian obligation to help such people achieve economic and social justice. Gustavo Gutierrez, a liberation theologian from South America, believes that Christians must involve themselves:

"in the protest against trampled human dignity, in the struggle against the plunder of the vast majority of humankind, in liberating love, and in the building of a new, just, and comradely society".

In other words Christians should:

◆ be liberators of the oppressed and disadvantaged as Christ was;
◆ give preferential treatment to the poor;
◆ establish communities in which people are treated equally and have power to make decisions about their own lives. In Latin America, Liberation Theology has inspired the formation of 'base-communities' made up of ordinary lay-people who attempt to apply the message of Christ in their own social situation. This may involve anything from building sewage systems to campaigning for street lighting.

Mother Teresa (1910-1997)

Mother Teresa was born in Yugoslavia and became a Loreto nun in 1928. She won international fame, including the Nobel Peace Prize, for her work among the destitute and poor of Calcutta. As a young novice arriving in India she was overwhelmed by the suffering, poverty

and deprivation in the slums of the city. After some years as a teacher she founded the **Missionaries of Charity** which is now an international organisation committed to working with marginalised people. Some of the work which Mother Teresa did involved supplying food, giving medical help and offering comfort to those who suffered. In everything that she did she kept in mind Christ's words:

"Whenever you did this for one of the least important of these brothers of mine, you did it for me."

Matthew 25: 40

In a TV documentary she once told the journalist Malcolm Muggeridge:

"The biggest disease today is not leprosy or tuberculosis, but rather the feeling of being unwanted, uncared for and deserted by everybody. The greatest evil is the lack of love and charity, the terrible indifference towards one's neighbour who lives at the roadside assaulted by exploitation, corruption, poverty and disease."

The Salvation Army

The Salvation Army was established in 1877 by **William Booth** and is dedicated to working with poor and underprivileged people. It is run on military lines and members, called soldiers, wear a uniform and belong to a 'corps'. They produce their own magazine, *The War Cry*, which they sell to members of the public to raise funds and publicise their work.

The Salvation Army is known worldwide and they have long established roots in Northern Ireland where they have a men's hostel, an old people's home and many churches.

They have also been known for many years for their music and bands.

A Salvation Army soldier in action

Activity

EITHER choose one of the above examples OR another Christian organisation that helps the marginalised and try to find out as much as possible about them. You could present your findings to the rest of the class in the form of a report or project.

Discussion

Organise a 'Paper Debate':
You will need:
1 sheet of A3 paper for each group
1 marker for each group
Method :
Divide your class into groups of four or five people. Each group will need a piece of A3 paper and a marker. Written at the top of each piece of paper will be a different statement from the list opposite. Each group will have two minutes to discuss the statement and write down an agreed response. The pieces of paper are then passed on to another group who respond to the statement and any previous comments. This continues until all topics have been discussed and responded to by all groups. At the end each group reports back the responses given to the question which originally started with them.

Questions

1 In what practical ways do you think the church could help marginalised people? Try to give FIVE examples.
2 Should the churches become involved in politics to try and bring justice and fairness to all?
3 In your opinion is violence ever justified when standing up against injustice or evil?
4 What does a Christian learn from the life of Christ about how to treat marginalised people? Give examples.

Statements:
★ God will help those who help themselves.
★ There are no really poor people in society.
★ Beggars have no dignity and should be cleared from the streets.
★ The National Lottery encourages addiction to gambling.
★ Alcoholics and drug addicts should have to pay for their own medical treatment.
★ AIDS is a judgement from God.
★ Ex-prisoners should be treated equally.
★ Special Needs schools should be integrated with mainstream primary and secondary schools.

Abortion

When a woman becomes pregnant an embryo is formed which has the potential to develop through all the stages of the human life-span.

If at any point the process of development is deliberately halted then an abortion has occurred. **An abortion is the intentional destruction of a foetus or the inducing of a premature expulsion from the womb to cause its death.**

The Law

Abortion is permitted under certain conditions in Scotland, England and Wales. The legislation which governs abortion in these regions is the **Abortion Act 1967** and **Human Fertilisation and Embryology Act 1990.** According to this, abortion is permitted if one of the following conditions is met:

a) There is a risk to the life of the mother.
b) There is a risk that the mother may suffer injury to her mental or physical health.
c) There is a risk to her existing children.
d) There is a strong chance that the child may suffer from serious mental or physical abnormalities.

Conditions b) and c) have a time limit of 24 weeks. However, the other grounds are permitted up to birth.

This legislation has proved controversial and unsatisfactory to both opponents and supporters of abortion. Anti-abortion campaigners say that some of the grounds for abortion, particularly the risk to a mother's mental and physical health and to her existing children, are social rather than medical and have in practice brought about 'abortion on demand'.

On the other hand supporters of abortion believe that the law does not go far enough and that abortion should be made more readily available.

At the time of writing, abortion in Northern Ireland is illegal. The legislation which is relevant is the **Offences Against the Person Act 1861.** It states that:

[go to page 56]

THE ISSUES

Pro-CHOICE

This is the name given to those who believe that abortion should be legal and freely available to those women who wish to terminate their pregnancy. One of the main pro-choice groups is **The National Abortion Campaign**. It believes that it is a woman's right to decide what to do if she is pregnant and it is involved in promoting its view through writing pro-abortion literature and asking politicians to represent its opinions.

Opinions

1. An embryo is a cluster of cells which is a potential human being, not an actual person.
2. Each woman should have the right to terminate her pregnancy if she wishes.
3. Abortion should be legal in order to prevent dangerous and unhygienic 'back-street' abortions.
4. An expectant mother may realise that the task of raising a child would be unbearable, and so it would be better if she did not have it.
5. Abortion should be available for women suffering under extreme circumstances, for example, if a woman becomes pregnant after being raped, or if the mother's life is at risk, she should not have to bear the child.

Pro-LIFE

This is the name given to opponents of abortion. The two main pro-life groups in the UK and Ireland are the **Society for the Protection of Unborn Children** (SPUC) and LIFE. These groups believe in the value of all human life, including the lives of unborn children. Their aim is to educate people about the wrongs of abortion, to lobby politicians and governments to implement 'pro-life' policies and laws. They also provide support and help for mothers and their children before and after birth.

Opinions

1. A human being exists from the moment of conception. This means that the single cell formed at conception has the potential to develop through all stages of the human lifespan.
2. All human life is of equal value — even a foetus or embryo has rights.
3. Less than one per cent of abortions are carried out solely to protect the mother.
4. The anxiety a mother experiences during pregnancy is not a reliable indicator of how she will feel once the baby is born. With help and support she may be able to cope.
5. Abortion is always evil and therefore should always be forbidden.

- no woman may attempt to 'procure her own miscarriage' using poison or any instrument;
- it is unlawful to assist any woman who attempts to have an abortion.

Supporters of abortion feel that the situation in Northern Ireland is inadequate because it is out of step with the rest of the UK. Those who really want an abortion can go to England to have one, but this means that abortion is only available to those who can afford to travel. Also, it makes a farce of the law if it is still possible to obtain an abortion even though it is illegal. On the other hand opponents of abortion say that there is no significant support for a change in the law in Northern Ireland as all the main political parties and churches oppose abortion.

What the Bible says

Christians see several references as relevant to the issue of abortion. On two occasions there is an indication that God considers an unborn child to be a living being:

"You created every part of me;
you put me in my mother's womb.
I praise you because you are to be feared;
all you do is strange and wonderful.
I know it with all my heart.
When my bones were being formed,
carefully put together in my mother's womb,
when I was growing there in secret,
you knew that I was there —
you saw me before I was born."

Psalm 139: 13-16

"When Elizabeth heard Mary's greeting, the baby moved within her. Elizabeth was filled with the Holy Spirit and said in a loud voice, "You are the most blessed of all women, and blessed is the child you will bear! Why should this great thing happen to me, that my Lord's mother comes to visit me? For as soon as I heard your greeting, the baby within me jumped with gladness."

Luke 1: 41-44

If it is accepted that an unborn child is a living person, then it follows that he or she deserves the rights and respect awarded to all human beings as the Bible teaches that all human life is sacred:

"So God created human beings, making them to be like himself."

Genesis 1: 27

One of the ten commandments clearly states: "Do not commit murder" (Exodus 20: 13), although in certain circumstances the Bible allows for the use of lethal force in self defence or in the defence of others. However, Biblical teaching states that the deliberate killing of an innocent human being is always wrong.

Furthermore, Christians believe that children hold a special place in the eyes of God. For example, Jesus said;

"Let the little children come to me, and do not hinder them, for the Kingdom of God belongs to such as these."

Luke 18: 16

There is one Bible passage which, some people suggest, implies that the foetus is **not** regarded as being as important to God as a grown human because the punishment for the killing of the unborn child is merely a fine whereas in all other circumstances murder is punished by death:

"If some men are fighting and hurt a pregnant woman so that she loses her child, but she is not injured in any other way, the one who hurt her is to be fined whatever amount the woman's husband demands, subject to the approval of the judges."

Exodus 21: 22

However, others point out that the crime relates to a miscarriage caused unintentionally, rather than through a deliberate act of abortion, and the fact that a punishment *is* given underlines the importance of the foetus.

What the churches say

There are certain basic facts about this issue that all Christian churches can agree with. For example, the statement by the **Presbyterian Church** that:

"The scriptures leave us in no doubt that from his earliest days in the womb, the unborn child is fully human, a person made in the image of God".

Leaflet on Abortion p 1

However, there do seem to be some differences of opinion when it comes to the question of abortion for victims of rape, or in the case of severe abnormalities in the foetus. The **Catholic Church** accepts that, in rare cases, certain measures aimed solely at curing medical conditions in an expectant mother may cause the death of an unborn child.

This is an unavoidable and tragic event, but the intentional termination of a pregnancy is always wrong:

"The direct and voluntary killing of an innocent human being is always gravely immoral."

and

"Life must be respected with the utmost care from the moment of conception. Abortion and infanticide are abominable crimes."

Gaudium et Spes 51. 3

The reason why abortion is wrong is because life is sacred and no human being may take another person's life unjustly.

"Human life is sacred because from its beginnings it involves the creative action of God and it remains forever in a special relationship with the Creator, who is its sole end. God alone is the Lord of life from its beginnings until its end: no one can under any circumstance claim for himself the right directly to destroy an innocent human being."

Congregation for the Doctrine of the Faith, Instruction Donum Vitae

The **Anglican** and **Methodist Churches** seem to suggest that there may be situations when abortion can be tolerated.

"We cannot emphasise too strongly the right to life and this includes the right of the yet unborn. The Lambeth Conference of 1958 received a Committee Report in which it was stated:
'In the strongest terms, Christians reject the practice of induced abortion, or infanticide, which involves the killing of a life already conceived (as well as a violation of the personality of the mother) save at the dictate of strict and undeniable medical necessity.'
This implies clearly that there can be medical circumstance in which a termination of pregnancy is required."

Statement from the Church of Ireland Standing Committee of the General Synod 1982, to the Taoiseach, Mr Haughey.

The Methodist Church is aware that the members of each congregation may have differing opinions on the issue of abortion but it tends to be the most open of the main churches in Ireland to the use of abortion, although this would still be in exceptional circumstances only:

"The worth of the human race itself hinges on reverence for human life at every stage and the long tradition of Christian teaching is marked by an
abhorrence of destroying the life in the womb. But a right to life does not mean an absolute right. Other lives have impinging rights. The life of the mother, whose survival may be crucial because care for the existing family depends heavily upon her, would appear to have priority over that of the foetus, if a choice has to be made.
"As a Church we are in favour of allowing the parties concerned to have the pregnancy terminated in the following cases: when there is grave risk to the mother's physical and mental health; when the pregnancy was the result of rape; when there is gross abnormality of the foetus."
From The Status of the Unborn, a report received by the Methodist Conference 1992

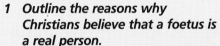

Questions

1 **Outline the reasons why Christians believe that a foetus is a real person.**
2 **Write a newspaper article entitled 'The Battle Over Abortion'. You should consider both sides of the debate and use examples from this chapter or from your own research to show what different pressure groups have to say on this issue.**
3 **Do you think there are any circumstances in which it would be difficult for a Christian to accept that abortion is wrong? Give reasons for your answer.**
4 **Imagine a female friend is twelve weeks pregnant. She is 16 and scared of the future. She comes to you for advice and wants to know what her options are. What do you tell her?**

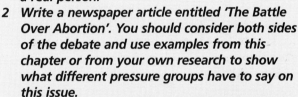

Discussion

Organise a class debate on one of the following slogans:

"God gives life, abortion destroys life"
"No to back street abortions"
"It is a woman's right to choose"
"Speak for those who have no voice"

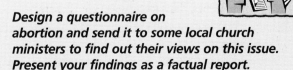

Activity

Design a questionnaire on abortion and send it to some local church ministers to find out their views on this issue. Present your findings as a factual report.

Euthanasia

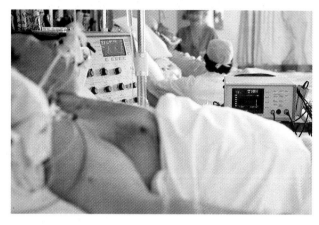

Euthanasia is the intentional ending of a life with the purpose of relieving suffering. **Euthanasia can be voluntary (at the request of the individual) or involuntary, (without the individual's consent).**

Voluntary euthanasia

Supporters of voluntary euthanasia (such as the Voluntary Euthanasia Society) argue that it is a humane act as it prevents a dying person from losing their dignity through suffering and it can also be a relief to families who experience anguish and distress by watching their relative suffering. They say it is an abuse of human rights to deny a person control over his or her own life. For example, when a person is very ill or frail they do not have the physical ability to take their own life and they should be allowed to ask a medical practitioner to do it for them.

Those who oppose voluntary euthanasia (for example, LIFE or SPUC) believe it is the deliberate killing of innocent human beings and is a violation of the right to life. They say that doctors should preserve life, not destroy it and that euthanasia presents several dangers to society. Firstly, if the idea that 'a life is no longer worth living' is accepted, we are saying that those who are ill or disabled are of less value than others. Secondly, a patient might request euthanasia simply because they are depressed or are put under unfair pressure by relatives. Thirdly, it must be remembered that doctors are not always correct in their diagnosis. A person can recover even after being told that they have only a short time to live.

It should be pointed out that opponents of voluntary euthanasia believe that euthanasia is **not** being practiced if:

◆ pointless treatment is withdrawn as it may even prolong the dying process;
◆ painkillers are given to reduce suffering but have the side-effect of shortening life.

In summary, euthanasia is always done with the *intention* of taking a life, and it is this deliberate act which is so controversial.

Involuntary euthanasia

Involuntary euthanasia is not openly supported by any group in Britain or Ireland, but it is still part of the debate on euthanasia. Anti-euthanasia groups argue that if euthanasia was made legal it would lead on to involuntary euthanasia. For example, a doctor may decide that a patient who is unconscious or in a vegetative state should have their tube-feeding withdrawn from them because they will not regain consciousness, but this would be involuntary euthanasia as the patient is not dying and cannot give their consent to the withdrawal of treatment.

The Voluntary Euthanasia Society do **not** support involuntary euthanasia either but say that voluntary euthanasia will not inevitably lead to involuntary euthanasia. They believe it is possible to make euthanasia legal without it being open to abuse by doctors or relatives of patients. They add that it is possible to safeguard against the misuse of euthanasia by ensuring that a second medical opinion and a psychiatric assessment is always sought and by the use of *Advance Directives* or *Living Wills* in which an individual specifies what should happen to them should various circumstances arise.

The Netherlands

Although there is no actual law in the Netherlands which states that euthanasia is legal, the situation is that a doctor will not be prosecuted if they follow certain guidelines:

◆ The request for euthanasia must come only from the patient and must be entirely free and voluntary.
◆ The patient's request must be well considered, durable and persistent.
◆ The patient must be experiencing intolerable (not necessarily physical) suffering, with no prospect of improvement.

◆ Euthanasia must be a last resort. Other alternatives to alleviate the patient's situation must have been considered and found wanting.

◆ Euthanasia must be performed by a physician.

◆ The physician must consult with an independent physician colleague who has experience in this field.

(Guidelines given by Mrs Borst-Eilers, Vice-President of the Health Council, Netherlands)

In 1995 a controversial programme about euthanasia in the Netherlands, *Death on Request*, was screened on the BBC. It showed a patient during his last days and the moment when the doctor gives him a lethal injection. Here are extracts from two newspapers which describe the programme and some reactions to it:

The Doctor prescribes Death

The patient is lying on his cot in the living room. He is too sick to get upstairs. He cannot breathe properly. The doctor leans over and speaks softly into his ear: "Do you really want to die?" Slowly, almost imperceptibly, the patient nods his head.

There is nothing left to him now but a slow and lingering torture, and fading memories of another life. He is weary of this existence. He has set himself for extinction and will embrace it, in order to preserve his dignity. "What can I offer that man?" asks the doctor, Wilfred van Oyjen. "What can I give him? You could give him drugs, but in the end it's only a stop-gap. There's no use. He's going to die and he knows it."

Cees, the patient, used to run a restaurant in Amsterdam with his wife Antoinette. Then he developed amyotrophic lateral sclerosis (ALS), an incurable, degenerative wasting of the muscles, also known as Lou Gehrig's disease. The illness progressed gradually at first, but suddenly overwhelmed him. His feet and legs became paralysed. The disease spread up his body, immobilising his right shoulder and arm, then spread to his face, partially paralysing his jaw and tongue, so that he could no longer speak properly.

Eventually, Cees was confronted with the full horror of his predicament: his mind, though fully conscious was trapped in a dying body. He felt like he was being buried alive. Unless he acted first, he faced an excruciating death by suffocation, as the wasted muscles of his chest finally collapsed and his lungs stopped working.

Cees asks Dr van Oyjen to kill him. Not once or twice, but again and again. The doctor must be convinced. There can be no room for whim or petulance in their mutual decision.

He growls at the doctor, his speech unintelligible to all except Antoinette, his constant companion and nurse. "He says we mustn't wait any longer," says Antoinette. Cees makes the noise again, a guttural slur. Then he hangs his head and sobs like a little boy, his numb shoulders shuddering with emotion.

The doctor is reluctant to kill a man, no matter how extreme his condition, but knows what he must do. "I've been asked," he says "and I feel I must honour that request. If I don't, I'm letting my patient down."

(From 'The Doctor Prescribes Death', Alix Sharkey, *The Independent*, Wed 1 Feb 1995)

The will is not to die but to flee

The most haunting image from the TV film *Death on Request*, shown last week, was not of the patient dying in Holland of motor neurone disease, nor of his wife. It was the anguished face of the Dutch GP, Wilfred van Oyjen, who administered the final injection to end his patient's life.

Out of the doctor's mouth came words to justify what he was doing. There was no alternative to ending his patient's suffering. But his eyes told a very different story. He couldn't sleep at night, nor could he bear to talk about the other patients whose lives he had similarly ended.

But in Britain at least, the choice is not between unbearable suffering and being put out of one's misery. The Dutch patient in this film was dying horribly because he was being left to suffer without any help. The GP said there was nothing he could do for him. The patient had been told he would suffocate to death. His pain and distress were therefore unendurable. There is a different choice in Britain. We now have considerable evidence that, with the development of hospices and palliative care, virtually all the distressing symptoms of terminal illness can be alleviated to the point were the patients who had wanted euthanasia no longer plead to be killed but make a good and natural death instead ...

According to Dr Nigel Sykes, a British expert in motor neurone disease at St Christopher's Hospital in London, not one of the 300 or so motor neurone patients treated at that hospice has ever suffocated. That symptom is simply alleviated.

The problem with voluntary euthanasia is first, that it may not be truly voluntary and that second, it leads inexorably to involuntary euthanasia. In Holland, it is performed not merely to end the distress of patients but because doctors are making value judgements about the quality of people's lives. The official Remmelink report in 1991 revealed that, in addition to 2,300 cases annually of voluntary euthanasia, there were a further 1,000 where patients' lives were terminated without their consent ...

Dutch practice is clearly out of control. But if anyone is surprised by these developments, if anyone thinks that euthanasia can be tightly controlled, they delude themselves.

(From 'The will is not to die but to flee.' by Melanie Phillips, *The Observer*, 19 March 1995)

The Hospice Movement

A Hospice is a centre where people who are terminally ill receive treatment and care. They are based on the belief that people who are dying can still have a high quality of life. This is achieved through the control of pain and through caring for the whole person — mind, body and spirit. Patients are offered support to face death. This involves medical staff, social workers and clergy. The idea is that the dying spend their last few days in a loving environment.

One of the founders of the Hospice movement was **Dame Cicely Saunders** who dedicated her life to helping people to die with dignity. She said:

"We have to concern ourselves with the quality of life as well as with its length."

On page 61 you can read an interview with a hospice nurse.

What the Bible says

To Christians all life is sacred and a gift from God (Genesis 1: 27). Also they believe that God alone has the right to take life:

"I was born with nothing and I will die with nothing. The Lord gave and now he has taken away."
Job 1: 21

The Bible teaches that suffering is not always a negative experience and it can, in fact, bring people closer to God. In the early days of the Church many Christians faced persecution ranging from confiscation of church property to torture and even death. Despite these dreadful circumstances the writers of the **New Testament** encourage the Christians to be strong and look at suffering in a positive way. For example:

"Trouble produces endurance, endurance brings God's approval, and his approval creates hope."
Romans 5: 3-4

"Be glad about this, even though it may now be necessary for you to be sad for a while because of the many kinds of trials you suffer. Their purpose is to prove that your faith is genuine. Even gold, which can be destroyed, is tested by fire; and so your faith , which is much more precious than gold, must also be tested, so that it may endure. Then you will receive praise and glory and honour on the day when Jesus Christ is revealed."
1 Peter 1: 6-7

Activity

Consider the following Biblical references. What do they say about the value of all human life?

Genesis 1: 27	Exodus 20: 13
Matthew 9: 18-26	Matthew 9: 35-36
Matthew 18: 12-14	Luke 12: 6-7

What the churches say

The **Presbyterian Church** chooses to emphasise care for the dying as opposed to practising euthanasia:

"Life is God's gift and the decision of how and when to end it is not ours to take ... Christians must get alongside those who are in pain or dying and show them the promise of life in Christ. We should be helping one another live through the dying process, not encouraging others to see a quick death as the solution."
Leaflet on Euthanasia

The **Church of Ireland** believes:

" No one has the right to take away the right to life, not even one's own ... So then, active euthanasia raises such major questions both for the medical profession and for the patient such as to make it morally unacceptable for a Christian."
General Synod 1993

They also point out that, if to continue with treatment of a patient is futile or hopeless, then it is not considered wrong to withhold the treatment. This is not considered to be euthanasia as the treatment is merely prolonging a natural death.

"It would appear that there is no moral imperative to the extension of mere physical existence beyond the point where the patient has lost any potential for a return to meaningful life, eg an irreversibly comatose patient. In such a state the patient is already well into the process of dying and no purpose is served by medical intervention which will serve only to prolong that process unnecessarily. The obligation is to ensure that the patient is made as comfortable as possible."
General Synod, 1993

Similarly the **Catholic Church** condemns euthanasia as 'morally unacceptable', and

"Discontinuing medical procedures that are burdensome, extraordinary, or disproportionate to the expected outcome can be legitimate; it is the refusal of 'over-zealous' treatment. Here one does not will to cause death; one's inability to impede it is merely accepted."
Catechism of Catholic Church para 2278

Joy Milliken nurses in the Marie Curie Hospice at Beaconfield in Belfast. During 1997 she was Northern Ireland's Nurse of the Year. In an interview with the authors of this book she talks about the work of the hospice and its approach to caring for the dying

What is a hospice?
At Beaconfield we have twenty three beds, three conservatory areas for patients and staff and a relative's room if any of them want to stay over. The unit is made up of a lot more than just doctors and nurses. They have a huge army of volunteers, over 100 volunteers, doing everything from cooking to gardening and offering a taxi service for patients taking them to and from medical appointments or bringing people to the day centre. We also have chaplains, two physiotherapists and social workers. In a hospice people are given the opportunity to live life each day as well as they can. They are given control of their own decisions and choices so that quality of life and dignity are not taken away. Patients come for respite care, symptom control and terminal care.

What does a hospice nurse do?
We attend to the physical needs of patients, sorting out any problems that may arise and give them their necessary medication. We spend time with patients and meet with relatives who sometimes need a lot of help to cope as well. If patients are dying we would, as far as possible, have a nurse with them, and solely with them and their family — our aim is not to have people die on their own. A lot of our patients are there to live, but unfortunately some are there to die as well and they all need the support and time we spend with them. Hospice nurses work as part of a team of staff. Every person has an important part to play. We care for the whole person — physical, social, spiritual and emotional.

What is the age range of your patients?
The youngest patient we've had in Beaconfield is 8, and we have from that up to 108.

How is a hospice funded?
In Northern Ireland, hospices receive about half of their money from the Health Authority, the rest has to be raised through donations. Funds would be raised through businesses, appeals, flag days and a lot of money would come in lieu of flowers at funerals. However, I don't think that it is right that a hospice should be a charity, it should be fundamental right. At the minute, one in three people is going to get cancer at some stage during their life and one in four is going to die from cancer, so if you are one of those one in four people you would want to know that provision is there to help you.

What are the main illnesses dealt with in a hospice?
Mostly cancer, I'm sure 95% of the illnesses treated are cancer. We also have had people coming in with AIDS-related illnesses and motor neurone disease.

What treatment do you offer the patients?
We have patients who have been referred purely for emotional support, who are not coming to terms with their illness. We have patients who need a lot of spiritual help and chaplains, along with other staff, would be very involved in counselling them. People also receive the medical treatment that they need. Usually many of the patients have had all the active treatment that they are going to get; they've maybe had as much chemotherapy or surgery as they can have, although they may be referred back again for radiotherapy or chemotherapy, but usually this is for palliative care. It's not to get a cure but to stop any problems or pain that might have arisen. People are treated regularly for infections; treatment is certainly not withheld from patients.

What are the arguments for caring for the terminally ill instead of helping people to die?
I think if people aren't receiving good terminal care then it's criminal. Hospice care has so much to offer so many. There is still a view that death from cancer is a painful, horrible and lonely way to die but there is no need for it to be if pain is well controlled and patients are well cared for. On the whole, people are not afraid of what is going to happen to them after they die; it's how they're going to die and the dying process that scares them. But drugs have improved beyond belief and most symptoms can now be well controlled — maybe not completely eradicated, but well controlled. Emotional pain can be a lot more difficult to deal with than physical pain and if you can get the emotional pain sorted out, get families together and get fears out of the way, you're halfway there. I don't think there is any argument for active euthanasia compared with terminal care. I think a lot of requests for euthanasia are due to a fear of loss of control and although a patient may be asking to die they would change their mind if presented with a syringe and told 'this is it'.

Questions

1 What is the difference between voluntary and involuntary euthanasia?
2 Using references from the Bible explain why most Christians are opposed to euthanasia.
3 What can hospices offer to dying people?
4 Write a letter to Wilfred van Oyjen, the Dutch doctor, giving your opinion on his actions.
5 "Care and understanding in the hospice movement and medical profession generally are constantly improving, but we still live in an imperfect world with no legal provision to confer absolute protection on the rights of the individual during the final chapter of life." (From 'The Last Right', Voluntary Euthanasia Society)
Do you agree that, while a hospice may provide care for the dying, people should still have a choice to request euthanasia if they so wish? Give reasons for your answer.

Activity

'In the Hot Seat!'

Each person in the class must be allocated one of the following roles:
★ A doctor who has carried out euthanasia on several patients.
★ A nurse who works in a hospice.
★ A patient who has a terminal illness and wants to have the choice of euthanasia if his suffering gets too much.
★ A priest or minister who objects to euthanasia.

When each person has been given a role they must write a short introductory speech and also prepare to answer questions from the viewpoint of their character.
The room is arranged with a single seat in the middle or at the front of the room. Each person (or as many as time allows) must take the 'hot-seat'. After giving their introduction they must take questions from the rest of the class. This is a very testing exercise and enables participants to gain an appreciation of a variety of perspectives on the issue, particularly if asked to defend a point of view which they, personally, don't hold.

Drug Abuse

Drugs in our society

When we use the word 'drugs' we are usually referring to illegal drugs such as cannabis or heroin but there are thousands of drugs in our society, both illegal and legal, and almost everyone in our society takes drugs in some form or another. There are three main groups of drugs:

Prescribed Drugs

Every day doctors prescribe thousands of drugs of various types in the hope that they will cure our aches and pains or ups and downs. The use of these drugs is strictly controlled — they are only allowed onto the market when rigorous tests have been carried out to establish the content of the drug and the exact effects of it on patients. The distribution of most medicines is carefully monitored by doctors and pharmacists so that they are taken correctly and only used for medical purposes.

Illegal Drugs

The Misuse Of Drugs Act (1971) states which drugs are illegal in the UK.

Drugs are classified as Class A, B and C in order of danger; these classes determine the maximum penalties for possession or supplying. Here are some examples:

Class A: LSD, ecstacy, cocaine, heroin, prepared magic mushrooms.

Class B: Cannabis, barbiturates, amphetamines.

Class C: Sedatives, tranquillisers.

The danger of buying illegal drugs is not only that you are breaking the law but you are taking an enormous risk. Illegal drugs are not subject to any official testing and in most cases the actual content and the exact effects of the drugs are not fully known. These drugs are sold by unscrupulous dealers who are not concerned for their customers health or welfare but are only interested in making money for themselves.

Alcohol and Tobacco

There is a final category of drugs, those which are not taken for medical purposes but are legal and freely available. These could be called 'legal, recreational drugs' and come in the form of alcohol or tobacco.

It is legal for a person of 16 years or over to buy and smoke cigarettes and for a person of 18 years and over to buy and drink alcohol.

The difference between these and illegal drugs is that the contents and side-effects of these drugs are well known. This does not mean they are harmless. On the contrary, they are both proven to be a risk to health but adults are free to choose whether or not to take them.

Why do people take drugs?

Humans have always been attracted to taking drugs. The reasons for this are many and varied and may depend on where a person lives or the culture to which one belongs. A group of 15 year olds in a class in Northern Ireland came up with the following list of reasons as to why they think people take drugs:

1 **Medical purposes** – When a doctor prescribes a drug he wants it to improve the health of his patient by reducing their pain and curing their illness.

2 **For pleasure** – The majority of people who take alcohol, tobacco or illegal drugs do so for pleasure; it makes them feel good. Often,

however, this pleasure is determined by the original mood of the drug user.

3 **To get high** – It cannot be denied that the initial effects of taking certain drugs are extremely exhilarating and exciting. The problem is that these feelings and sensations do not last.

4 **To fit in** – Taking drugs can help people to be more sociable. Inhibitions are removed and people feel more at ease in mixing with others.

5 **Lessens anxiety and depression** – People who find it hard to cope with the pressures of everyday life often feel they need something to prevent anxious feelings or even depression. Tranquillisers are often prescribed by doctors to serve this purpose.

6 **Religious/Spiritual reasons** – Certain religious groups encourage drug taking to deepen religious experience. Cannabis is often smoked to help meditation and encourage deep mystical experiences.

Another reason why some young people take drugs is because they are influenced by their friends to do it. This is called **peer pressure**. The following story shows how easy it is to get caught up in taking drugs even for those who think they will always say 'no'.

'Just a little pick-me-up...'

Janice was excited. She couldn't believe it when Mum said it was okay to stay over at Andrea's house. She'd been invited to a club in Belfast by two girls she worked with. It was her 'A' level year but the money from her part time job at the new supermarket was coming in handy. She felt grown up — working, clubbing. Soon she'd be at university and school, homework, nagging teachers would all be a thing of the past.

There was a huge queue already forming when the three girls got to the club. The L.A., like other clubs was well tuned in to the dance culture. Janice was fascinated when, after paying their £10 admission, they found themselves inside with hundreds of people hugging and dancing like crazy on the dance floor, full of E and full of energy. They looked like the happiest people she had seen.

"Look", Andrea shouted through the music, "I've spotted Kevin. Give us £15 each and I'll get us something to last the night."

"How do you mean?" Janice asked nervously.

"Just a little pick-me-up," Siobhan smiled, getting out her purse.

"Come on, it'll save us buying drink all night."

Janice was torn. She'd read the horror stories about people who had died taking ecstasy. She'd always been dead against it.

"Janice, there's no harm. Look at everybody. Do you think they are high on life? Come on, I know Kevin, he wouldn't give us anything dodgey."

Janice handed over the money and looked around her. The people who took Ecstasy seemed to know what they were doing and they were all looking after each other. Nothing really bad would happen. Andrea soon returned and the three of them then went in to the toilets.

Twenty minutes later they became part of the crowd, dancing and sweating on the spot, (it was roasting on the dancefloor). The DJ saluted the crowd telling them to "Go, feel the groove". The lights flashed in sync with the beat, about 130 beats a minute. Janice felt exhilarated and fantastic. She didn't even know who she was dancing with — it didn't matter, She loved them anyway.

Janice felt a tugging at her shoulder. It was Andrea. "Janice, give me some money for water. Siobhan is about to faint!"

"I've none left!"

The two of them stumbled off the dance floor. Siobhan was sweating and shaking on the edge of the floor. Andrea looked horrified as they watched Siobhan collapse to the ground.

It seemed like seconds later when an ambulance arrived and paramedics were attending to Siobhan.

The DJ tried to bring the level down a bit, slowing the speed. Andrea and Janice left with the ambulance. They were still shaking.

"Why wasn't it me?" This thought turned over and over in Janice's mind. One of the paramedics looked at them sternly. "We think she'll be OK ... this time" he said and turned back to Siobhan. Janice thought about what lay ahead ... police, their parents, friends. What had she done?

Activity

1 **What made Janice, who was so against drug taking, take ecstasy at the L.A. Club?**
2 **Why did the drug not have the same effect on all three girls?**
3 **If you were a policeman/woman dealing with the three girls, what would you say to them the next day?**
4 **Janice did not experience any real bad effects of taking ecstasy this time. Do you think the whole experience will have convinced her not to take drugs? Give reasons for your answer.**

Discussion

Discuss the following questions in small groups and then report your opinions to the rest of the class:

Is there such a thing as a sensible amount of alcohol?

When does drug taking become drug abuse?

"If drugs were legalised it would be easier to control their use and there would be less drug abuse." Do you agree or disagree? Give reasons for your answer.

SOME COMMON DRUGS
AND THEIR EFFECTS

Name	Type	Class	Effect
Alcohol	Depressant	legal	Reduces inhibitions, enhancing the ability to socialise. Drinking too much can cause vomiting, dehydration and 'hangover'. Many people feel over-sensitive or even aggressive. It is the cause of more violent and criminal behaviour than any other drug.
Cannabis	Depressant Hallucinogenic	illegal class B	Relaxing; enhanced aural awareness; midnight snacking; giggling; can weaken short-term memory over a period of continual usage; mixes badly with alcohol; four times more likely to cause cancer than tobacco.
Ecstasy	Stimulant Hallucinogenic	illegal class A	Intense euphoria and energy; feelings of intimacy; ability to dance for hours. Nausea, diarrhoea; sweating; tiredness and depression. Death caused by respiratory collapse or overheating.
LSD	Hallucinogenic	illegal class A	Trips which can last up to twelve hours, visual hallucinations intensifies all feelings and sensations both good and bad; flashbacks; paranoia.
Tobacco	Stimulant	legal	Gives a buzz; may reduce stress; soothing; tastes good after a meal; addictive; increases risk of heart disease, cancer, and bronchial infections.

Taking any drug involves a certain amount of risk. Therefore, the more frequently a person takes a drug the more they are exposed to its dangers. But drug abuse is not limited to those who take drugs over a long period of time. It can also be a single event and occur on a single night. The fact is that drug abuse is much more common than we might think. A patient who takes a tranquilliser prescribed by their doctor to alleviate anxiety or sleeplessness may have psychological problems or even become addicted if they use them for a long enough period or in large enough amounts. Similarly 'social drinkers' put themselves at risk if they become drunk; they can become over-sensitive, aggressive or even violent. They may also vomit and suffer dehydration.

In both of these cases, the individual is abusing a drug and causing themselves to experience unpleasant and dangerous after-effects. Although each case of drug abuse is different, there are some common effects on the individual and society. Here are some of the areas in which problems can occur:

Financial

Even moderate use of drugs is expensive. From buying a pack of cigarettes to feeding a heroin habit costs a lot of money. Often other expenses and bills are put to one side and this can lead to serious debt.

Work

The side effects from some drugs can prevent a person from doing their job properly. Absenteeism or irresponsibility at work can lead to loss of employment which then creates a poverty trap from which an individual can find it hard to break.

Health

Taking a drug will inevitably have an effect on the body, but this will vary from drug to drug and person to person. Every drug has its own dangers — smoking may cause breathlessness and eventually cancer; sniffing glue can cause sickness, damage to heart, kidneys and lungs and even death due to heart-failure, choking on vomit or suffocation.

Relationships

Cannabis, ecstasy, LSD and alcohol are all examples of drugs which can change a person's mood or personality and can make them feel sensitive, aggressive or paranoid. These changes obviously have an effect on how drug-users relate to other people around them and can cause conflict, emotional trauma, separations and violence.

What does the Bible say?

The Bible makes a few brief references to alcohol which suggest it can be used in a positive way:

"Do not drink water only, but take a little wine to help your digestion, since you are ill so often."
1 Timothy 5: 23

"Produce wine to make him happy."
Psalm 104: 15

However, there are also a number of references which suggest that a Christian should not condone the use of illicit drugs, alcohol or tobacco. Biblical teaching continually underlines the fact that we should care for our own bodies and view our health as a gift from God. In the New Testament Paul sees the body as a Temple of the Holy Spirit (1 Corinthians 3:16-17; 6:19) and as such we should not consume anything which would cause us harm. The Bible also stresses the importance of looking out for others and setting a good example.

Discussion

Look up the following references and then discuss what you think they say about responsibility for ourselves and responsibility for others:

1 Corinthians 3: 16-17
1 Corinthians 10: 23-11: 1
Luke 10: 27
1 Corinthians 8: 13

What the churches say

Church teaching on this issue focuses on the concept of responsibility. **Methodists**, for example, believe that:

"Because of the nature of Christian love, there is the obligation to exercise responsibility towards the use of creation, towards other people in community and towards oneself."
Statement by Council on Social Welfare on Alcohol Abuse.

The **Presbyterian Church** teaches that drugs can '*steal your mind*' when your mind should be used to:

"improve our relationship with God and other people. In this way, you will be 'transformed by the renewing of your mind' (Romans 12v2)."
Understanding HIV/AIDS, Alcohol and Drug Education Committee

As a result, the Presbyterian Church feels that its members should abstain from taking any drugs, including alcohol:

"The General Assembly, in the light of medical evidence and recognising that, in the New Testament, Christian liberty is limited by love of one's neighbour, and recognising also that both the moderate drinker and the weaker brother can be put at risk by the use of alcohol, recommend all their members to adopt and commend a policy of total abstinence."
The Presbyterian General Assembly 1979

Finally, some churches point out that the immorality in drug abuse is not just in the actual taking of the drugs themselves but also the way in which illicit drugs are traded. For example, the **Catholic Church** states:

"Clandestine production of and trafficking in drugs are scandalous practices. They constitute direct co-operation in evil, since they encourage people to practices gravely contrary to the moral law."
Catechism of the Catholic Church para 2291

Drug prevention

Drug prevention is a social strategy which incorporates various organisations, agencies and institutions such as health authorities, youth clubs and schools. These groups are all concerned with contributing to the education, reduction and prevention of drug and alcohol consumption.

In practice drug prevention involves:

- discouraging people from experimenting with drugs in the first place;
- attempting to stop the problem and the harmful effects it causes;
- acknowledging, in some cases, that people do take drugs and lessening the risks involved.

One of the methods which is increasingly used in drug prevention is **peer education**. This involves young people being taught about drugs and their harmful effects, by others of their own age. There is evidence which suggests that this approach, at the very least, delays young people from experimenting with drugs and may prevent it in some cases.

Case study — Ballymena YMCA

"Broad Range is a peer education project run by the Ballymena YMCA in county Antrim. It is concerned with the benefits of young people educating other young people to the dangers of drugs. Broad Range carries out suitable programmes for various groups and organisations such as schools, churches and youth clubs. Broad Range believe that peers are more likely to have the kind of credibility with young people that may be difficult for a professional worker to acquire. Messages are more likely to be listened to if those delivering them appear easy to identify with. Friendship groups are formed and in these groups young people learn from each other about the dangers of drug use."
YMCA leaflet on Broad Range

Activity

Imagine you have been asked to participate in a peer education project on drug prevention. Prepare a speech or design a poster which could be used as part of the drug prevention programme.

WOrk

'True Romance' Brad Pitt

Work plays a fundamental role in our community. It is the foundation on which the structures of our society are built. By working we *occupy* and *employ* ourselves and at the same time help to keep our society running in an organised way. The importance of work is also seen in the way that it affects all other aspects of our lives. There is a strong connection between the type of work you do and how long you will live, where you live, how much money you have and who you marry. Work is a basic element of our existence.

The nature of work is something that has undergone dramatic changes through the centuries. In earliest times, work and survival were the same thing, everyone being occupied with growing food or hunting animals. However, as humans developed their skills, they began to specialise in particular activities; some people provided a service or a particular skill in return for food or payment. People became dependent on one another and societies grew more organised. We now live in a highly developed and inter-dependent society where the majority of people are employed in very specialised activities of which relatively few are concerned with farming the land.

According to sociologists, we are now living through the era of the technological revolution. Whereas in the past employment was provided for the majority of people by large, industrial firms,

Social Responsibilities

The poet John Donne wrote, "No man is an island." By this he meant that our lives are affected and influenced by others around us and whether we like it or not we are never entirely independent but need and rely on other people. In order for a community or society to function successfully its members must co-operate and accept that everyone has certain rights and responsibilities. The right to work is probably the best example of this. Everyone deserves the opportunity to find fulfilment through work, but with this comes the responsibility to contribute positively to the society in which they live.

The huge cranes at Harland and Wolff's shipyard are a familiar sight on the Belfast skyline.

there are now many smaller companies who employ fewer people and who depend heavily on computer and robot technology to carry out many of their tasks. In 1900 Harland and Wolff, a Belfast-based firm, was a world-leading builder of ships. Thousands of people worked there to help make Belfast a prosperous city. The linen industry was also a huge employer in Ireland and had international fame. These were **labour-intensive** jobs which meant a lot of people were required to make the final product. Nowadays, the linen industry has virtually disappeared and, while Harland and Wolff still exists, it employs many fewer people than it did previously and has had to make many changes to adapt itself to the new working environment. The development of technology has, therefore, meant that many people who worked in traditional industries like ship-building, linen or coal-mining have been made **redundant**.

On the positive side, the technological revolution has made businesses more efficient and has also created opportunities for a new generation of young people who have been educated and trained for work in this new environment.

Alongside all these developments, changes have also been taking place in the way people work. No longer do the majority of people work from nine to five, five days a week, in a job which they will keep for life. Rather the world of employment has become a much more flexible place.

◆ More employees work irregular hours.
◆ Part-time work and job-sharing are common.
◆ Employers prefer to issue short-term contracts.
◆ Governments encourage self-employment.
◆ Technological advances mean that more people can work from home.

Why do people work?

There are many reasons for work. Here are a few:

Money – This allows us to provide for our basic needs of food, clothes and housing but also gives us the opportunity to enjoy leisure activities outside work.

Social interaction – Work is an important source of relationships outside the family.

Fulfilment – Work provides us with a sense of identity, a role within society and a sense of personal achievement when a job is well done.

Organisation – Work divides the day and week into time periods which help us to organise our time effectively and purposefully.

Creativity – We can also achieve a sense of purpose as well as satisfaction from developing our skills and being creative.

Discussion

In groups discuss:

1   **What type of work do you think you would like to do in the future? Describe your ideal job.**
2   **What expectations do you have of what work will mean to you?**
3   **Do you think there is a danger in judging people according to their work rather than who they are?**

Real lives

A variety of people in different types of employment speak about why work is important to them.

Aine, 25, is a social worker.

"One thing I really like about being a social worker is dealing with a great variety of situations. I work, in particular, with families and young people who are experiencing difficulties — from cases of truancy to instances of child abuse. This provides me with a great challenge, although the intensity of the work can sometimes be stressful. I can gain a lot of reward from seeing people succeed in coping with their problems. Of course, my job also provides me with an income which maintains me in a very satisfactory lifestyle."

Billy, 60, is a school technician in a Technology department.

"My work gives me an interest and brings me satisfaction. Working in a school environment provides me with a great variety of tasks — from doing maintenance, liaising with teachers to helping pupils. When I'm working I enjoy having an organised routine as it helps me direct my time both inside and outside work."

Alastair, 32, is a European marketing manager.

"My job is to sell technical products developed in Northern Ireland to European car companies like Mercedes, Renault and Peugeot. So I get plenty of opportunity to travel, meet and work with people of different cultures. It's a very challenging job which requires communicating a detailed knowledge of our product in several languages. There are rewards however. I enjoy working as part of a team and socially interacting with other people. Financial reward was initially very important to me in my job but the longer I work the more I see that all-round job satisfaction is the most important thing."

Christian attitudes to work

The Bible has many things to say about the whole area of work. One of the main points it makes is that the skills we possess for our work are God-given gifts. For example, in the **Old Testament** Isaiah attributes the farmer's skill to God's grace:

"He knows how to do his work because God has taught him."

Isaiah 28: 26

Likewise in Exodus we read of God's hand in creative skill:

"God has filled him with power and given him skill, ability and understanding for every kind of artistic work."

Exodus 35: 31

Work is therefore seen as something good because it is part of normal life designed by God. In Jewish culture it was not unusual for work to be one of the main priorities of a person's life:

"Then people go out to do their work and keep working until the evening."

Psalm 104: 23

Vocation

Christians often talk about being *called by God* to do a particular job. There are examples of this in the Bible when Abraham, Moses, Jeremiah, St Paul and St Peter were asked to do something for God. So Christians today believe that God can still call them to do a particular job or task; this is described as receiving a **vocation**.

The word 'vocation' can describe a specialised calling, for example, the call to be a priest, a minister or a missionary.

Kenneth Clarke outlines his calling to this type of vocation and explains how he became a Church of Ireland clergyman:

"God calls us. He puts his word into our hearts and it becomes like a burning fire. It has to be proclaimed. It is released when we obey and the fire becomes a blaze. This is how all Christian ministry begins. It begins with God. The ordained ministry is not by self-appointment but by Divine appointment ... it is a heavenly call to responsive, obedient hearts ...

"In my own life I reached the point where I had to take some initial steps in the belief that, if I wasn't hearing God accurately, then at some point during the process of selection [for the ministry] he would close the door. I stepped out in faith, asking him to stop me if it was not his will. At each point the doors opened. We are aware of a Divine nudge to which we are obliged to respond. It is the Holy Spirit working within us."

Called to Minister Church of Ireland Evangelical Fellowship, Booklet 7

'Vocation' can also be used to describe more everyday occupations. The caring professions (such as nursing, teaching or social work) in particular, are called vocations because they require a genuine concern for people, which arises out of a desire to serve God and others, as Christ did. However it is possible for *all* Christians to feel a vocation for the work they do if they work for the glory of God. Paul says:

"Whatever you do, work at it with all your heart, as though you were working for the Lord and not for men."

Colossians 3:23

Rights and Responsibilities

It is recognised in law, and also in the Bible, that employers, employees and consumers all have rights and responsibilities.

Employers

An employer should pay workers a fair wage for the work that they do. This means that workers should not be exploited or cheated out of money by being given less than they deserve. It is a well-known fact that many of the goods in our high street shops, from trainers to rugs, are manufactured with cheap labour in foreign countries and sold in this country at a massive profit. Charities such as Oxfam campaign against such exploitation and have introduced their own 'Fair Trade' brand of products which includes coffee, sugar and craft goods. The workers who produce these are paid a fair price for their labour so that their communities can afford healthcare, education and food.

The Bible teaches that an employer should not discriminate against anyone on the basis of their gender, religion or race. Discrimination can involve not giving equal pay, conditions or opportunities to all workers equally. In the **Old Testament** it is made plain that this is a sin:

"Do not cheat poor and needy hired servants, whether fellow-Israelites or foreigners living in one of your towns. Each day before sunset pay them for that day's work; they need the money and have counted on getting it. If you do not pay them, they will cry out against you to the Lord, and you will be guilty of sin."

Deuteronomy 24: 14-16

Employers should provide safe working conditions for their employees. Places of work, particularly in heavy industries, can be extremely dangerous. Men and women can be seriously injured or even killed as a result of an unhealthy or dangerous working environment. Employers in Europe are under obligation to provide proper safety equipment and take appropriate precautions to avoid any risks to the health of their employees. Over and over again the Bible also reminds us of the value of the individual and the sanctity of life.

Another aspect of Biblical teaching on the role of an employer is that the employer should not cheat consumers out of money when selling their product.

"The Lord wants weights and measures to be honest and every sale to be fair."

Proverbs 16: 11

Today weights and measures are not as easily tampered with as in the past. However, the command that every sale should be fair is still applicable. Misleading packaging or inaccurate advertising are the modern-day equivalents to faulty weights and measures.

In conclusion, Christians believe that it is wrong for an employer to be involved in any type of work which makes money unfairly or which takes advantage of people in any way:

"Do not take advantage of anyone or rob him. Do not hold back the wages of someone you have hired, not even for one night."

Leviticus 19: 13

Employees

Being a responsible employee involves putting Christ's teaching to love your neighbour as yourself into practice. Christians should consider both their work colleagues and employers as 'neighbours', towards whom they should adopt a loving attitude.

Here are some examples of how this might be done in the workplace:

◆ **Be honest** — for example, start and finish at the correct time, don't take for personal use what belongs to your employer.

◆ **Work for God's glory** — always work to the best of your ability.

◆ **Show respect for those in authority over you** — don't always be moaning about your boss and complaining about their decisions. Instead be co-operative and not disruptive.

◆ **Do not judge others** — healthy working relationships require tolerance, patience and forgiveness. Everyone makes mistakes or wrong decisions so do not be quick to condemn others.

Finally, the Bible shows that along with the right of the individual to earn money comes the responsibility of using it wisely. For example, Paul showed that working hard enables people to help those who cannot earn enough themselves. When he addressed the Elders at Ephesus he encouraged this kind of attitude:

"I have shown you in all things that by working hard in this way we must remember the weak, remembering the words that the Lord Jesus himself said, 'There is more happiness in giving than receiving'."

Acts 20: 35

Paul suggests that a company or an individual should not be selfish with their profits but be prepared to share them with others.

Trade Unions

The Trade Union movement was started in the nineteenth century by those who wished to prevent exploitation of workers. Working conditions were appalling — factories were not safe, employees could be dismissed without a fair reason, women were discriminated against and children exploited. A single worker was powerless against a factory owner who wanted to keep wages low and profits high. Early Unions were merely collectives of workers who gained some bargaining power through the strength of their numbers.

Today's Unions continue to represent and support workers. They believe that everyone is entitled to:

◆ work
◆ decent conditions
◆ security of employment
◆ fair pay
◆ the right to join a Union

If it judges that its workers are not being treated fairly then it will campaign to employers or government for change. However, if their bargaining fails, they may have to resort to other action to put further pressure on the employers. A few examples of Trade Union actions are:

◆ one-day strike
◆ all-out strike
◆ overtime ban
◆ work to rule (when workers withhold their goodwill and work exactly to their contract)
◆ go-slow
◆ sit-in
◆ picketing

Questions

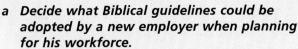

1   Make a list of occupations which you would describe as being 'vocations'. Give reasons for your choice.
2   A nurse in the Third World once said: 'A vocation is its own reward.' What do you think she meant by this? Do you agree?
3   Do you think it would be difficult to be a Christian and work for a business which makes a lot of money?
4   Read the following passages:
a) Colossians 3: 23. What should a Christian's attitude be to their work? Consider the word 'vocation' in your answer.
b) Ecclesiastes 3: 22. What do you think makes a person happy in his or her work?
c) Amos 5: 10-15; 8: 6. What type of behaviour does God condemn which ignores people's rights and responsibilities?

Activity

In groups:

a   Decide what Biblical guidelines could be adopted by a new employer when planning for his workforce.
b   Use these guidelines to draw up a charter outlining the rights and responsibilities of both employer and employees in a small supermarket.
c   A male employee has been seen leaving work an hour early, for the third time this month, by a fellow church-goer. She decides to confront him about his behaviour and remind him of how Christians should act in their place of work. Roleplay the conversation between the two.

UNEMPLOYMENT

In the previous chapter, we have seen how work occupies a central place in people's lives. This will help us to understand the seriousness of being unemployed. People can believe they are worth nothing; it may seem that they are no longer contributing to the general life of their community and they may experience awkwardness or conflict with their family. They have to endure enforced leisure simply because they have nothing else to do and they may begin to feel they have no purpose to their lives.

What causes unemployment?

Unemployment can occur for a variety of reasons and can be linked to national, local or personal causes. Below are some typical reasons:

◆ People are competing for jobs and there are simply not enough to go round.
◆ Workers lack the appropriate skills or qualifications to fill vacancies.
◆ Job losses can be caused by technological developments which mean a machine can do the work instead of a human.
◆ A person may be unemployed for a period between leaving one job and starting another.
◆ A country or community which experiences civil unrest will have difficulty attracting business and employment.
◆ There are a small number of people who may prefer unemployment to work.

Effects on individuals and their families

Case study

One unemployed man, Peter, from County Tyrone, described what it felt like when he lost his job:

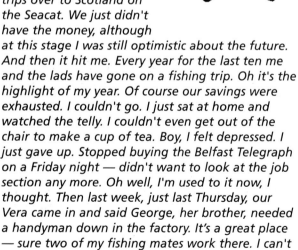

"When I lost my job — I was a caretaker down in the primary school — it was awful. Y'know, I felt bereaved; it was like losing a relative or a good friend. I was shocked. I'd worked there for 20 years. Who'd take me on now? I'm a middle-aged man! I just couldn't take it in. After a few weeks of doing nothing except visit that dole office I became really angry. How dare they make me redundant after all the overtime I'd put in, at Christmas and all! I tell you my self-confidence had taken a bitter blow. And then there was the wife — the rows we had over that first few months. She still wanted her new sofa and trips over to Scotland on the Seacat. We just didn't have the money, although
at this stage I was still optimistic about the future. And then it hit me. Every year for the last ten me and the lads have gone on a fishing trip. Oh it's the highlight of my year. Of course our savings were exhausted. I couldn't go. I just sat at home and watched the telly. I couldn't even get out of the chair to make a cup of tea. Boy, I felt depressed. I just gave up. Stopped buying the Belfast Telegraph on a Friday night — didn't want to look at the job section any more. Oh well, I'm used to it now, I thought. Then last week, just last Thursday, our Vera came in and said George, her brother, needed a handyman down in the factory. It's a great place — sure two of my fishing mates work there. I can't wait to get back to work!"

Questions

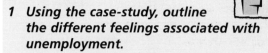

1 **Using the case-study, outline the different feelings associated with unemployment.**

2 **Make a list of positive things Peter could have done while he was waiting for a new job.**

3 **Some people believe it is possible to feel creative and useful without having a regular job. Do you think this is idealistic? Give reasons for your answer.**

4 **Politicians have suggested that the workless can serve the community by improving the environment, eg gardening in public parks. Do you think Peter would have benefited from this sort of scheme? What are the advantages and disadvantages?**

5 **One of the effects of unemployment mentioned by Peter was that he suffered from depression. Sometimes being unemployed can lead to depression because a job brings you a sense of purpose and direction. Read the following article and make a list of the effects unemployment can have on the individual and their family.**

"A substantial proportion of the unemployed live in poverty surviving only on minimal state benefits. The longer unemployment lasts the deeper the poverty ...

Besides financial hardship, the unemployed are likely to suffer many other misfortunes. They are less healthy than the employed. They are also more likely to get divorced: increased conflict between husband and wife is regularly reported by the unemployed, quarrels arising partly because of worries about money, partly because of the demoralisation of unemployed men in particular. Boredom, sickness, sleeplessness, isolation, anxiety and loss of self-confidence are among the main complaints normally associated with a period of unemployment."

(*Contemporary British Society* 2nd Edn N Abercrombie and A Warde, Polity Press, 65 Bridge St Cambridge, CB2 1UR, 1994)

The effect on the community

Unemployment can have a very negative effect on a society or community and create unsatisfactory conditions for those out of work and those left in work:

1 The unemployed may look for a scapegoat for their situation and blame vulnerable or weak groups in society for their predicament, for example, ethnic minorities, the disabled or women. As a result racial tension can arise and violent behaviour can occur.
2 If the effects of unemployment on the individual include depression, divorce and violent behaviour, then the subsequent effect on the whole society will be to undermine the stability of family and increase levels of crime.
3 Reduced prosperity will have a knock-on effect within a small area and local businesses will lose trade as people won't be spending as much money.
4 Those left in work may feel less secure and therefore unable to leave an unsatisfying job or ask for a pay increase. As a result the working population becomes frustrated.

Christian attitudes to unemployment

During the 17th century an idea grew up around the teaching of **John Calvin** which came to be called the **Protestant work ethic**. Calvin, a Protestant leader, believed that work was a religious calling and an essential duty in a Christian's life, made necessary by Adam and Eve who were forced to work after they were expelled from the Garden of Eden. Calvin and his followers understood work as a punishment to be endured, but which should be carried out with a single-minded determination. As a result anyone who was without work was considered lazy and ungodly.

This view, however, is not shared by all Christians as they see work as something which provides self-fulfilment and needs to be balanced with leisure. The **Methodist Church** regards the Protestant work ethic as simplistic because an attitude which demands that all people *must* work encourages judgement of those who can't work or are unable to find work and therefore:
"takes no account of the fact that for over 20% of the population of Northern Ireland there is little or no choice with regard to gainful employment".
Poverty and Deprivation, 1991

Other Christians agree that the Bible does not condemn those out of work, as the majority of people who are out of work would love to find a job. There is a huge difference between being redundant and being lazy. In the book of Proverbs we read that:

"Some people are too lazy to put food in their own mouths."
Proverbs 26: 15

People are lazy when they do not want to work even when they have the opportunity to do so. This is what Paul was referring to in his second letter to the church at Thessalonica:

"While we were with you we used to say to you, 'Whoever refuses to work is not allowed to eat'."
2 Thessalonians 3: 6-13

Do you think Paul's teaching is relevant today?

How can churches help?

The church has a vital role to play when it comes to unemployment. Jesus taught that the Kingdom of God was for everyone and not just for the well off or those perceived to be blessed. The church, therefore, should be active in all aspects of community life, including the downside.

Churches in Co-operation is one organisation that works to help the unemployed in the north-west of Ireland. It was set up in 1983 and involves the four main churches — Church of Ireland, Roman Catholic, Presbyterian and Methodist — in the Derry/Donegal area. The organisation has more than 300 volunteers who are involved in many types of community projects, from helping the elderly to improving the community in which they live.

Churches in Co-operation also:

◆ sends unemployed people, from both communities and both sides of the border, to America each year to develop new job skills and to get to know each other;
◆ trains and recruits volunteers;
◆ helps establish other community groups such as Foyle Victim Support Scheme;
◆ assists in overseas projects in Russia and Africa to help with community work there.

In the future Churches in Co-operation hopes to establish a Youth Forum and a local council of churches in Londonderry. It is also taking the lead in creating an urban park within the city walls.

Churches in other areas have also tried to help those who are unemployed. They have responded positively to the problem and have opened their doors to invite community initiatives into their buildings. Coffee mornings, drop-in centres, libraries and crèches are but a few of the ways in which local churches are attempting to help. **Job Clubs** involve local Christian businessmen giving help to church members when it comes to filling in application forms or writing up a curriculum vitae. Others help create jobs such as gardening, decorating or odd jobs to help build up a person's experience. People gain a sense of self-respect from work that matters. They may not necessarily get paid, but knowing they have helped an elderly person from the congregation may be a reward in itself. Older people may be able to offer classes to teach secretarial skills. There is a wealth of experience in many churches which can be drawn upon.

Activity

Look at the following list of different ways in which the church can help the unemployed stay active and gain experience. Draw a table distinguishing between the activities you think would be practical and those which simply would not work in a church in your area.

Home improvement	Gardening
Car maintenance classes	Growing vegetables
Car boot sale	Writing/poetry classes
Visiting sick or elderly	Baby-sitting
Wood work	After school club
Holiday Clubs	Knitting
Craft shop	A church library

Make a poster which could be displayed by the local church in a community to advertise to unemployed individuals the activities you have chosen.

Discussion

You have probably discovered that, with a bit of effort, there is a lot a church could do. What do you think are the three most practical suggestions? Give reasons for your choice. Is there anything listed which you think is unsuitable? Can you think of any other ways in which the church can help?

Questions

1 **What do you think the churches' role should be in a society which has increasing unemployment figures? Give reasons for your answer.**
2 **How can the church teach that we are all of equal value in God's eyes, whether we have a job or not?**
3 **Structured Essay:**
   Your Uncle Jim has become unemployed. He is married with three children. Susie (17) is sitting her 'A' level exams next year. Martin (11) will be starting secondary school in September and Sabrina is only six weeks old. Martha, your aunt, worked part-time in a shoe shop in town but she gave up her job after the baby was born. The family are regular church goers.
(a) *What effect will unemployment have on*
      Uncle Jim
      Aunt Martha
      the children
(b) *Suggest ways in which the various members of the family can help with the situation in a practical way.*
(c) *How best can Uncle Jim make the most of his time?*
(d) *How can the local church help in this situation?*

THE VALUE OF LEISURE

The average person works a 40 hour week, although there are obvious exceptions. The time that is left over after we have done our day's work can be called leisure time. During this time we carry out various activities other than work. These can range from reading a book to playing sport or watching TV. Everyone spends their leisure time in their own unique way.

Discussion

Look at the following list. Does it include any of your favourite leisure activities?

Football	*Walking the dog*
Reading	*Computer activities*
Baking	*Drawing/painting*
Swimming	*Watching TV*
Mountain biking	*Horse riding*

Make a list of the most common leisure activities for those of your age group.

Paul is 16 years old and attends school in Belfast. Here he describes how he spends his leisure time:

"After working hard at school I really enjoy going to football training on Wednesday nights and playing for the team on Saturdays. I find that sitting at a desk most of the day makes me really tired so it's really important for me to do regular physical activity to keep fit and help me relax. Of course, I really enjoy spending time with my friends at the weekend as well. We usually go to the cinema or play snooker which is always a good laugh. If I get fed up doing homeworks during the week and need to switch off I would watch TV for an hour or so, take Rocky, our alsatian, for a walk or play a game on my computer. I hope that when I leave school and get a job I'll always take time to relax. I really believe that you should work in order to live, not live in order to work."

When people work hard, leisure is particularly essential. You may well remember a popular advertising jingle for the chocolate bar Mars: "A Mars a day helps you work, rest and play." Most people would agree that we need a balance of these three things in order to stay healthy and able to enjoy life to the full.

Sports in particular can be a good leisure activity because they:
◆ keep you physically active and fit;
◆ encourage perseverance and team spirit;
◆ help you to interact with others;
◆ develop skills;
◆ give responsibilities to those with leadership qualities.

A Christian view of leisure

The **Calvinists** of the seventeenth century had quite clear ideas about leisure. Leisure time was frowned upon as time-wasting which encouraged laziness, gossip and more sleep than was necessary. The only value of sport and recreation was for improving one's health. Anything that was done purely for entertainment, such as theatre going, drinking or dancing were regarded as sinful.

Attitudes in the Christian church are now, on the whole, radically different from this puritanical approach. Christians today recognise that life is a gift  from God and should be enjoyed — so valuing our leisure time should be very important:

"I have come in order that you might have life — life in all its fullness."

John 10: 10

The Bible suggests that leisure enables us to work better. In the **New Testament,** Jesus shows

A History of Sunday

"He blessed the seventh day and set it apart as a special day."

Genesis 2: 2

"Observe the Sabbath day and keep it holy"
Exodus 20: 8

✚ Early Christians shared with Judaism the belief that as God rested one day in seven so should they. However, they changed the day of rest from a Saturday to a Sunday, mainly as a commemoration of the day that Christ rose from the dead.

✚ In the fourth century, the first Christian Emperor, **Constantine**, made Sunday a special day by forbidding all townspeople to work.

✚ After the Reformation, during the seventeenth century, a movement called **Sabbatarianism** encouraged extremely strict interpretation of Sunday as a day of rest which meant no work, no sports and no entertainment.

✚ In 1781 an Act of Parliament, *The Lord's Day Observance Act* made it illegal to open a place of entertainment on a Sunday.

✚ In 1831 the *Lord's Day Observance Society* was founded by Anglicans.

✚ *The Shops Act* of 1950 stated: "All shops must close on Sunday except for certain transactions ..." This act was still in force in 1991 when major chain stores in the run up to Christmas disobeyed the law by opening on Sunday.

✚ In 1997 a new law was introduced: *The Shops (Sunday Trading) (NI) Order*. This allows small shops to open all day on Sunday and large shops to open between 1pm and 6pm on Sunday. It also attempts to protect workers' rights by ensuring that shop workers are not compelled to work on Sundays against their wishes and that a worker cannot be dismissed for refusing to work on a Sunday.

us the importance of a balance between work and rest when he visited Mary and Martha.

Read Luke 10: 38-42

On this occasion Martha was scolded for letting her work become too important to her. Mary, however, was praised for allowing herself to relax and listen to Jesus' teaching. This concept is also reflected in the book of Ecclesiastes where the Philosopher concludes:

"All of us should eat and drink and enjoy what we have worked for. It is God's gift."

Ecclesiastes 3: 13

Leisure is also important because it brings people together. For example, families and friends meet or make trips to participate in their favourite leisure activities. Christians also stress the importance of spending time with friends. Fellowship has always been important to the Christian faith and indeed Jesus himself often took time off to spend with his closest friends:

"So he said to them: 'Let us go off by ourselves to some place where we will be alone and you can rest for a while'."

Mark 6: 31

Sunday: a day of rest

Sometimes working too hard can make us feel rundown and burnt out. Resting or taking time to unwind can help us feel restored mentally and physically and ready to face the world again. That is why Christians place so much importance on keeping Sunday special as a day for rest and relaxation, as well as worshipping God.

Christians don't share a common view on how Sunday should be spent. They agree that Sunday should be set aside as a day of worship and a day of rest, but there is no agreement on what constitutes rest. A few Christians hold a **Sabbatarian** point of view which regards any non-essential work as wrong. Other Christians consider anything which is leisurely, from sports to shopping, as a valid way to spend Sunday. On the whole, churches allow their members to exercise their own judgement on this issue. For example, the **Church of Ireland** states:

"The official position of the Church of Ireland is that Sunday is to be reverently observed as the Lord's Day

Sunday Trading

FOR

- Jesus taught "The Sabbath was made for the good of man; man was not made for the Sabbath". This means you should do whatever you enjoy doing on a Sunday.
- Everyone should be able to choose for themselves whether to shop or not.
- Shopping is a form of leisure.
- Shopping provides more part-time jobs.
- For those who work six days a week it may be their only time to shop.
- Hours of trading (1 pm to 6 pm) don't interfere with the usual times of church services.

AGAINST

- Trading on a Sunday disregards God's law to keep one day holy.
- If some people choose to shop on Sunday it destroys the idea of a day of rest for everyone.
- Workers may have little choice about working on a Sunday and be threatened with the sack if they don't co-operate.
- Christian employees may find it difficult to 'fit-in' if they refuse to work on Sundays.
- Sunday is the only day when both children and parents are completely free to spend time together.
- Resting one day in seven is a physical necessity.

... Christians have a duty on Sunday to join with their fellow Christians in corporate worship, but leaves to the conscience of the individual how exactly the remainder of the day is spent. Sunday is to be used as a day in which Christians renew themselves in mind, body and spirit, always remembering that in so doing they must endeavour to avoid causing disturbance to their fellowmen."
Role of the Church Committee, 1974

Discussion

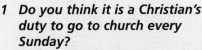

1 **Do you think it is a Christian's duty to go to church every Sunday?**
What activities would you regard as inappropriate on a Sunday?
In your opinion, what is the best way for a Christian to 'renew themselves in mind, body and spirit'?

2 **"Today there is leisure in abundance but it would sometimes seem that we have lost the ability to be leisurely; with the possession of motor cars and motorcycles, hours of restfulness have become hours of restlessness, and if the lack of these vehicles precludes one from rushing away in order to rush back again there is the wireless to distract the mind and the television to rivet the attention to the exclusion of all else — even of one's own friends."**
(Sidney Macer-Wright)
Do you think there is any truth to this statement? Give reasons for your answer. What would you consider to be worthwhile and worthless leisure activities? Would you like to have more leisure time or do you think you can have 'too much of a good thing'?

Questions

Read Mark 2: 23-28 and answer the questions below.

1 **Why did the Pharisees criticise the disciples on this occasion?**
2 **Explain how Jesus justified his actions in verses 25-26.**
3 **How did Jesus' reply answer the criticism of the Pharisees?**
4 **Many Christians regard Sunday as a special day arguing that the Old Testament law forbids all but essential work. Do you think this is still relevant in our society? Give reasons for your answer.**
5 **Look at the following reasons for leisure:**

Rest	Exercise
Develops talents	**Relaxation**
Socialising	**Prevents boredom**

a) What do you think is the most important reason for leisure?
b) Would you add anything to this list?
6. **"Leisure is a God-given right." Do you agree? You should refer to Biblical teaching in your answer.**
7 **Some people think of unemployment as enforced leisure and view the prospect of a day with nothing to do as more stressful than a hard day's work. Do you think this is true? How might someone who is unemployed still value their leisure time?**

Activity

Organise a class debate using one of the following motions:
"This house believes that Sunday Trading is unnecessary" or
"This house believes that shopping on Sunday is another form of leisure."

INdeX

Page numbers in **bold** indicate a major reference